» Simple Guides
HINDUISM

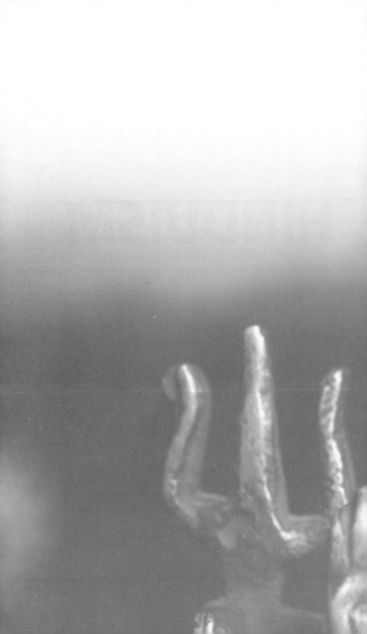

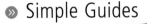
» Simple Guides

HINDUISM

Venika Mehra Kingsland

Published in Great Britain by
Simple Guides, an imprint of Bravo Ltd
59 Hutton Grove, London N12 8DS
www.kuperard.co.uk
Enquiries: office@kuperard.co.uk

First published 1997 by Global Books Ltd.
This edition published 2008

ISBN 978 1 85733 437 1

British Library Cataloguing in Publication Data
A CIP catalogue entry for this book
is available from the British Library

Printed in Malaysia

Cover image: Statue of Shiva – creator, preserver and destroyer.
istockphoto/Tjasa Maticic
Drawings by Irene Sanderson

About the Author

VENIKA MEHRA KINGSLAND was born and brought up in India in a privileged, traditional, Hindu family. Her mother, Radhika, is both a devotee and, with nearly ninety years of study, one of the widest read of Hindu women. Through her mother, Venika was able to know, and learn from, many of the most significant Hindu figures of the twentieth century, including Poddarji, creator of Gita Press, Swami Ranganathananda, President of Ramakrishna Math, Swami Chinmayananda, and Swami Digvijayanath of Gorakshanatha Math.

During the 1960s Venika helped renew Indian interest in yoga when she taught leading film stars and wrote for popular magazines. In the 1970s, Dr Ramamurti Mishra, Sanskritist and neurosurgeon, and Sri Navajata, Chairman of the Aurobindo Society, wrote forewords to *Complete Hatha Yoga* and *Hathapradipika*, which she co-authored with her husband. In addition, Venika was co-founder of the Centre for Human Communication in both the UK and USA.

I would like to acknowledge with gratitude the endless hours my husband Kevin spent tirelessly questioning me about my deeply held beliefs.

This work is dedicated to my son Kris and the generation he represents, whom I hope the profoundly inspiring message of Hinduism may reach.

⊙ Contents

List of Illustrations

⟩ Preface

Any attempt to share an inside view of Hinduism draws on Sanskrit (meaning 'complete, elegant, exact'), which belongs to the Indo-European family of languages. This speech-group includes Greek, Latin, most of the modern European and Northern Indian languages, as well as the ancient and modern languages of Iran. As Sanskrit is a precise language it is not always easy to find an exact English equivalent; the original words, therefore, have been used whenever appropriate. The Sanskrit used today is written in a script called *Devanagari* ('alphabet of the gods'), which is also used to write Hindi, the official language of India. Hindi derives many of its words from Sanskrit.

The vernacular spellings of Sanskrit words have been used (without the diacritic, or accent, marks) throughout this book, following the accepted practice of most Hindus when writing in Roman script. The Glossary contains the transliterated Sanskrit spellings in parentheses where they are very different. All Sanskrit words are written in *italics* the first time they occur in the text.

The name of Rama in Sanskrit

Approximate English equivalents are given in
parentheses or in a footnote if more appropriate.
Words that have become part of the English
language, such as Buddha, Calcutta, guru, etc. are
exempted. Sanskrit proper names are written with
initial capitals, although this is not customary as
Devanagari does not have capital letters.

The most ancient texts were composed in Vedic
Sanskrit, which is closely related to Old Persian.
Later texts were compiled in classical Sanskrit.
Many of these texts have been translated into the

principal Indian languages, as well as a variety of other languages, with varying fidelity. These days, Sanskrit is mainly used for the more formal Hindu ceremonies and rituals.

It is hoped that this book will be welcomed by those readers who are interested in Hindu thought and practices. It should be especially valuable to those who come into contact with Hindu communities and are seeking a deeper understanding of Hindu culture. In writing, I have been particularly mindful of those Hindus who have been born and brought up in the West or have received a Western-style education in India and may have lost direct contact with traditional Hindu thought. Unfortunately, no account can encompass every subcultural view and this book is inevitably written from a North Indian perspective. For this I must take full responsibility.

The principal aim of this guide is to provide a fresh yet authentic insight into the rich variety of religious traditions that are collectively known as Hinduism. The brief history and background of the evolution of Hinduism, including the contribution made to it by other cultures, should provide the reader with a sense of its complexity. Together with its deep underlying simplicity, Hinduism is a metaphor for our times.

VENIKA MEHRA KINGSLAND

⌃ Elephant god Ganesha, son of Shiva and Parvati

⊙ Introduction

In thinking about Hinduism, it is natural to think about India. It is often assumed that Hinduism is India's state religion and that its origins are there. However, neither assumption is quite correct. India is a secular country, although Hinduism is practised in one form or another by the majority of its people (over 80 per cent). In contrast, Hinduism is the official religion of Nepal where around 90 per cent of the population are Hindus. In fact, Hinduism has also been practised for centuries in other parts of the world (chiefly Southeast Asia, Indonesia, East and South Africa). In recent times, it has spread with the general diaspora of Hindus to Europe, North America and Australasia.

The word 'Hindu' is the Persian form of the Sanskrit word *sindhu* ('river, ocean') used by Persians (pre-fifth century BCE*) to refer to people beyond the great river Indus (itself a later latinized form of the same word). Indo-European peoples who had entered the region applied the word to the delta of the great river (it is now Sindh province in Pakistan). Later,

* BCE (Before the Common Era) = BC, CE (Common Era) = AD

⊙ *Hindu procession in London*

when Persia was conquered by Arabs and Islamized, and Muslims subsequently conquered Sindh (in the eighth century CE), the word Hindu was adopted by them to designate the non-Muslim population.

Hinduism is an all-embracing word for a very involved system. Some might argue that it is not a single religion, but at best an association of religions. Yet, despite the apparent diversity, there are many common features which are shared by all Hindus.

Viewed by outsiders, it is a complex phenomenon with seemingly contradictory beliefs and a countless number of gods. Viewed from within, most Hindus believe in a singular God. For them Hinduism is a way of life that they grow up with and follow, often without question. They adopt the traditions that are prevalent in their own family and maintained by intermarriage within a small number of families.

Language in Hinduism is rich in metaphor, heavily endowed with symbol and significance. A Hindu is usually born into this rich cultural heritage and it requires a conscious effort to explain to the uninitiated what is taken for granted. This tradition encompasses the discourse of sacred literature and rigorously preserved oral texts, within a powerful non-verbal cultural context. None of these components alone is sufficient for understanding as all three together mutually specify meaning. Thus, a number of terms and ideas are interpreted afresh in this book in an attempt to convey the deep meaning they hold for the developed Hindu mind.

In the past, few spiritually rich cultures have attempted to share their knowledge with outsiders, although some proselytizing cultures, notably Christianity and Islam, have succeeded in asserting religious hegemony. However, in the emerging global economy the cultural treasure houses are cautiously being opened. Spiritual jewels that have been carefully preserved by Native Americans, Australasians and Asians in particular, are now being glimpsed by a world community to the enrichment of all. Some Hindu temples are literally built above treasure houses packed with gold, silver and precious jewels.* But this is nothing compared to the lasting spiritual wealth they have preserved.

* My brother was privileged to view and value many of these temple treasure houses for insurance purposes.

Chapter 1

Gods & Deities

Hindus believe in one God, Brahman, the Supreme, One without a second, the Singularity. Brahman is described as *nirguna* – without any attributes. However, just as all human beings have their own perspective, they may also have their own personal or individual god. These gods are described as being *saguna* – with attributes.

The individual need not be restricted to one god. Different gods have different attributes and you choose one for the occasion. For example, Ganesha, portrayed as the elephant-headed god of wisdom and remover of obstacles, is always invoked before the start of a new venture. Lakshmi is seen as the goddess of wealth for bestowing riches, and the goddess Sarasvati as imparting learning. Such personification of the worshippers' perspective of God is rather like, though not the same as, the Christian tradition of asking a saint to intercede on one's behalf.

The rich Hindu imagination has given concrete form to aspects of the mind. The many faces of reality are depicted by rich imagery. For example,

⊙ *Brahma – the creator*

the *Trimurti* (three images or material forms) symbolizes three aspects of this Brahman, the ultimate ineffable reality. Brahma is the creator and the first member of the trinity. Vishnu is the sustainer, whilst Mahesh, the third member of the trinity, is the completer or destroyer and is more popularly known as Shiva.

From ancient times storytellers and artists have used symbols to depict specific attributes of the deities. Detailed rules are laid down in texts on iconography, some dating from the fifth century CE.

⊙ *Parvati and Shiva standing in front of the* shivalinga *(phallic symbol) as creativity. Many temples are devoted to the* shivalinga

Necessary skills are acquired and passed on by apprenticeship. Thus, deities are given different forms, such as number of arms, which depicts their powers. Specific gestures portray various attitudes. For example, a hand with the palm facing the worshipper and fingers pointing down portrays a nurturing aspect, whilst protection is implied when the fingers point upwards. In the same way specific items placed in the hands of the deity indicate attributes and spiritual meanings. Deities are also visualized as having distinctive colours, which draw upon a highly developed aesthetic tradition. An in-depth explanation of the symbols is beyond the scope of this book but readers are invited to reflect on them to bring the meaning alive for themselves.

Brahma

As Brahma plays a major role only in the beginning of the world cycle he is thought to be in meditation the rest of the time. Given this aloofness he is not one of the popular gods. In some traditions he was virtually co-existent with Brahman, the divine source of ultimate reality and was also the first man – Manu Svayambhu. His consort is Sarasvati, the goddess of learning, and his vehicle is often depicted as a swan. Although he is the first member of the trinity he is

sometimes depicted as sitting on a lotus rising from
Vishnu's navel. This symbolizes an interdependency
versus a hierarchy of the gods. In some myths he
was depicted as having five heads and one of these
was cut off by Shiva.

Vishnu

Hindus generally fall into three broad groups of
adherents. The first is comprised of Vaishnavites, the
followers of Vishnu. Vishnu is normally depicted
with four arms: one hand holds a lotus; a second
holds a conch (which may be blown like a trumpet);
a third holds a discus (which always returns by itself
after being thrown); the fourth carries a mace. The
petals of the lotus are believed to symbolize the
unfolding of creation; the conch symbolizes the
cosmic vibration from which all existence originates.
The discus and the mace were obtained by Vishnu
as rewards for a victory over the god Indra. His wife
is Lakshmi, goddess of beauty and fortune. Together
they form an entity called Lakshmi-Narayan. He
rides a huge creature, half bird and half man, called
Garuda. His home is in a heaven called Vaikuntha
(from which Ganga – the sacred Ganges river – is
believed to flow, its source at Vishnu's feet).

Vishnu, a lotus emerging from his navel, can be
shown resting on the coils of *Sheshanaga* (the

cosmic serpent), which floats in the cosmic ocean. Sheshanaga's coils represent the repetitive cycles of time. Sometimes shown as encircling the earth, Sheshanaga also symbolizes eternity. Vishnu sleeps on the coils during the cosmic night between the last dissolution of the universe and its new manifestation (see The Brahmanic Time-Scale in Chapter 6, page 66).

Vaishnavites include worshippers of Vishnu's important avatars (incarnations), Rama and Krishna. Each time Vishnu incarnates so does Lakshmi. Thus, when Vishnu became Rama she incarnated as his wife Sita, and then as Krishna's wife Rukmini. Also included in this group are the followers of Hanuman, represented as the monkey god, who is best known for his devotion to Rama.

Krishna

Krishna is probably Hinduism's most popular god. He is often depicted as surrounded by a group of *gopis* (cowgirls) and most often with one gopi, Radha – a married woman. The gopis', and particularly Radha's, love for Krishna has been developed into a metaphor for the love of God and is the subject for many devotional and sometimes erotic songs. Radha-Krishna, as the couple are known, are to be found in countless paintings, sculptures and icons. They are central figures in many dances and plays. Krishna is depicted as dark blue in colour and usually has a flute in his hand.

Shiva

The second group of adherents consists of the Shaivites – Shiva's followers. Shiva takes many forms. The best known are Pashupati (champion of animals) and Nataraja (king of the dance). As Nataraja he is depicted as having four arms: one holds a hand drum controlling the rhythm of the universe, the second beara a flame of the fire of purification, the third offers protection and the fourth salvation. He dances the *tandava* – symbolizing the continual dance of creation and dissolution involving the whole cosmos, the basis of all existence and of all natural phenomena. This is believed to be the motivation for temple dancing, seen particularly in South Indian temples. The *devadasis* (maidservants of the gods) used to dance to please gods and pilgrims. Such dancing today finds expression in the classic Bharata natyam (*Bharat* – India, *natyam* – dance) style.

In other representations, Shiva is portrayed as the god of asceticism, with matted hair, naked and smeared with ashes. He is occasionally depicted with a third eye in the middle of his forehead. This is usually closed and is devastating when opened. It signifies wisdom which comes from alternative and more inclusive insight. He is also shown with snakes around his neck, with a trident as a weapon and riding his vehicle, Nandi (enjoyment), the bull. The bull with its character of power and potency represents *dharma* (righteousness, justice and moral order).

Shiva is often symbolized by the *linga* (the male organ) as creativity and many temples are devoted to the *Shivalinga*. The will of Shiva is manifested by the power of his Shakti, his female partner Parvati, who also has many other forms and incarnations. Shiva's linga is the cosmic creative organ which needs to be placed in a receptive female organ, a *yoni*. Traditionally, this is the only way to channel this all-powerful creativity which otherwise could be destructive.

Shiva is very much admired by women (despite his hairstyle) and is regarded as the ideal role model for a husband. He is characteristically loving and generous to his wife, treating her as a companion, helping her to develop, yet holding her in reverence. Shiva has always been considered a 'soft touch'. He is prone to grant boons to anyone who asks, often without considering the consequences (and thus has to be bailed out by Vishnu). Chanting his 1,008 names is, in itself, considered an act of worship.

❯❯ Shakti and the Durgapuja Festival

In the Shaivite tradition, the female principle of creation and the mother goddess is known as Shakti. She is worshipped in her own right, not merely as a female partner or wife. (The description of Shakti as power is rarely applied to other goddesses such as Lakshmi and Sarasvati.) The Shakti cults (the followers are called Shaktas), which form the third group of adherents, pertain to Shiva's wife Parvati. She is Durga in Bengal, and her visit to her family and return to her husband Shiva are celebrated every October.

The festival is called Durgapuja and the whole of the city of Calcutta practically closes down for about ten days. Images of the goddess are created out of *papier-mâché,* then cast into the Ganges in a dramatic midnight ceremony resounding with drums and glowing with candles. In Bengal, Durga rides a tiger, although this is exchanged for a lion in other parts of the country. In different incarnations she is Kali (black) and Sati (pure). Among her other titles are *mata* (mother) and *devi* (goddess).

Symbols

 This Sanskrit character is pronounced *aum*, sometimes written *om*, and found inscribed on buildings, vehicles and texts all over India. It is one of Hinduism's most sacred symbols and regarded as an important *mantra* (*man* –

mind, + *tra* – protect). Mantras are verbal expressions, a sacred word or phrase, usually drawn from sacred texts, Vedic verses. The dot (*bindu*) in the aum symbolizes a transcendental state beyond space and time. It represents an ineffable realm beyond the capabilities of the discursive mind, reflected in the *chandra* (half moon). Its triple components (shaped like the number '3') portray the beginning, maintenance and dissolution of the universe and it also stands for the three gods Brahma, Vishnu and Shiva.

The *swastika* (self-energetic), as a cross, is an ancient symbol and in many cultures it is a symbol for inherent dynamics, especially those in living systems. It is in the form of a cross with the ends of its cross-bars bent to the right or left, indicating rotation or spin. For Hindus the right-facing swastika is associated with Vishnu and Ganesha. It also represents the four human accomplishments (see page 54), brings luck and is often seen painted above the entrances of homes. The left-facing swastika has negative connotations.

Bindi
Bindi is derived from *bindu* – spot, drop or globule. This is commonly seen as a red mark on the foreheads of women. Certain Brahmin priests have

recognizable markings on the forehead, depending on the sectarian group to which they belong. Generally, vertical marks are applied by the devotees of Vishnu and horizontal ones signify allegiance to Shiva. Applying the traditional bindi to the forehead is part of ritual worship and is of particular importance during the Hindu marriage ceremony. Materials used include a red powder, ash, sandalwood paste or saffron. Each has a different meaning and is used at different occasions. Today, the bindi has also become a fashion item for women and can be obtained from most marketplaces as a 'peel and stick' item in a myriad of colours and designs.

» Facets of God

Brahman – the Supreme, One without a second, Singularity

Trimurti – the three facets of Brahman, manifesting as:

Brahma	Vishnu	Mahesh/Shiva
Brahma the creator. His female partner is Sarasvati, goddess of learning.	Vishnu the sustainer has twenty-two incarnations, of which the best known are the following ten: Matsya Kamath Varaha Narasimha Vamana Parashurama Rama (Sita*) Krishna (Rukmini* and Radha*) Buddha Kalki Vishnu is also known as Narayan; his wife is Lakshmi, goddess of wealth, and his female form is Mohini. * The female partner	Mahesh, also known as Shiva the completer or destroyer, has 1,008 names, including: Rudra Shankara Natraja Neelkantha Pashupati He is sometimes symbolized by the linga (the male organ) as creative energy; there are many temples devoted to the Shivalinga. His female partners include: Maheshvari, Sati, Parvati, Durga, Shakti, Kali and Kami Devi.
		Shiva and Parvati have two sons: Kartikeya (his vehicle is a peacock) is also known as Skanda; and Ganesha, depicted as the elephant god. Ganesha's wife is Riddhi-Siddhi, and his daughter is Santoshi Mata.
	Hanuman is portrayed as the monkey god and is a devotee of Rama.	

Chapter 2

History

The **Indo-Europeans migrated** to the Indus valley region of the Indian subcontinent from the north-west, evidence suggests, during the second millennium BCE. They arrived over several hundred years in numerous waves. We know that the subcontinent was already home to groups of Negrito, Proto-Australoid, Mongoloid and Mediterranean people.

The Vedic Period

These Indo-Europeans referred to themselves as *Arya* or Aryans (literally, elevated, noble or honourable). They were part of the great Indo-European family which spread from Europe through central Asia and shared a common language and culture. Their religious heritage bore similarities to the ancient Greek, Roman or Celtic belief systems. They brought with them a great textual tradition that we have come to know as the *Veda* (*Veda* –knowledge, from the root *vid* – to

⊙ *The divine couple: Shiva and Parvati*

know). Veda is the summary name for a collection of scriptures sacred to the Hindus. The period up to the time of Buddha is known as the Vedic Period. It is popularly thought of by some groups as a glorious age of the distant past when heroic figures upheld righteousness.

The Aryans were organized into three *varnas* (societal groupings): *Kshatriya* – kings, warriors and technologists; *Brahmin* – historians, educators and priests; and *Vaishya* – people who worked on

⊙ *A composite of Durga (mother goddess) and Lakshmi (goddess of wealth). She rides a tiger, Durga's traditional vehicle. Also in the picture is Hanuman, who is followed by Skanda (Kartikeya), Shiva and Parvati's son*

the land and artisans (now extended to include traders of goods and finance workers). These groups were similar to the tripartite division of ancient Indo-European society, as evidenced in Greece and Rome. They were not originally hereditary. Nor were there any rules limiting social

interaction or marriage between these classes.
Struggles for dominance between local groups
characterized this phase of Aryan expansion.

Vedic culture steadily declined and, by about the
sixth century, conditions were ripe for reform movements. By this time Northern India had at least

sixteen well-articulated political units. Some were kingdoms and others were essentially tribal republics. Group loyalties promoted the divinity of the king supported by the priests. The relationship between the Brahmins and the Kshatriyas became complex: on the one hand it was synergistic and on the other they vied with each other for power.

The republics retained much more of the earlier tribal tradition than did the monarchies. There was, however, a parting with Vedic orthodoxy and various new sects emerged, including Buddhism and Jainism. These were to become important religions. Gautama (566–486 BCE), the founder of Buddhism, was born in Kapilavastu, in the modern Kingdom of Nepal. Buddha was an oral teacher; he left no written body of thought. His beliefs were categorized by later followers.

Buddha's Four Noble Truths

Buddha's enlightenment was the realization of the Four Noble Truths:

(1) Life is suffering – Buddha accepted the Vedic idea of life as cyclical, with death leading to further rebirth. (2) All suffering is caused by ignorance of the nature of reality and by attachment. (3) Suffering can be ended by overcoming ignorance and attachment.

(4) The way to transcend suffering is by the Noble Eightfold Path.

The aspects of the Path are divided into three categories that form the basis of Buddhist teaching – morality, wisdom and *samadhi* (concentration). Buddhists maintain that by destroying greed, hatred and delusion, which are the causes of suffering, one can attain *nirvana* (enlightenment).

Vardhamana, who came to be known as Mahavira (the great victor), was the founder of Jainism. He was an older contemporary of Buddha and came from the same part of India. The Jaina (from *jina* – to conquer, hence Jainism) practise the Five Great Vows:

Ahimsa (non-violence) in every aspect of life
Satya (truthfulness)
Asteya (refusal to steal)
Brahmacharya (sexual restraint)
Aparigraha (being non-grasping)

They believe that the material world is eternal and progresses endlessly in cycles. Jainism takes a strikingly austere view of purifying oneself.

Both founders were Kshatriyas and had been deeply influenced by the Veda. Both religions were to have a significant historical impact. The founder of the Mauryan dynasty, Chandragupta (322 BCE), became a Jain and his grandson Ashoka became Buddhist. We see a revival of these ideas several hundred years later in the mainstream of Hinduism.

After Alexander the Great

The Mauryan dynasty flourished in the vacuum left earlier by Sekunder (Alexander the Great, 356–323 BCE), and reached its zenith under Ashoka. Emperor Ashoka's India had advanced agriculture and an elaborate administration and tax-collection system. Having converted to Buddhism, Ashoka abandoned the policy of military conquest in favour of the victory of righteousness. His ethical teachings are found inscribed on pillars and rock-faces all over the subcontinent, where his empire extended. His emissaries travelled far and wide, including to the Hellenistic kingdoms and Sri Lanka. Buddhism was dominant for over a thousand years.

The Mauryan dynasty did not survive very long after Ashoka's death. Many of the kingdoms in the north decayed. Around the second century CE the Seleucid Greeks and other nomadic marauding peoples swept in from central Asia. They were followed by the Sakas (Scythians) and later the Kushans (Tocharians). Kushan emperors and Greek feudatories often adopted Sanskrit names and followed some of the local religions. In turn, the influence of Hellenistic culture is evident in Gandhara.*

Various groups arrived, each contributing ideas to this melting pot of cultures. Indeed, Alexander the Great was so impressed by the high quality of the indigenous Ayurvedic (science of life) medicine that he took physicians and practitioners back with him to the West. This later returned to India as Unani – Greco-Arabian medicine – with the Muslims. It still flourishes side by side with Ayurvedic, modern medicine and other traditions.

Other religions also arrived, including Christianity. It is traditonally accepted that the apostles Saint Thomas and Saint Bartholomew established Christianity in South India during the first century. The Syrian Christians of Malabar claim that they were evangelized by Thomas, who was killed by a spear and buried at Mylapore, near Madras.

Around this time the Indo-Aryans expanded into Sri Lanka and South-East Asia. Despite small thrusts made by various predatory groups, including the Huns and the Arabs, Northern India enjoyed several centuries of respite from foreign aggression. For over four centuries the squabbles were internal.

* A region in the north-west of India called Gandhara in ancient times and now including Afghanistan and part of the Punjab, it has given its name to a Graeco-Buddhist school of sculpture that combined the influence of Greek forms and Buddhist subject-matter.

First Sultanate in Delhi

The eleventh century CE saw the establishment of the Sultanate in Delhi by the Turkish Mahmud of Gazni. Mahmud directed his attacks at the great temple towns, specifically Somnath in modern Gujarat, which was particularly wealthy. Apart from the riches that were plundered, iconoclasm was considered a meritorious activity by orthodox Muslims. The non-Indo-European influence began to dominate and Islam was introduced by force. It occupied more or less the same territory held by Buddhism, which was effectively replaced on the mainland of the subcontinent.

Tribal and clan rivalries culminated in the sixteenth century with an invitation to the great Mughal warlord Babar. North India was taken over by the Mughals (Mongols), descendants of the fearsome nomadic warriors. They had destroyed everything in their path as they poured forth from Mongolia in the thirteenth century, but had been civilized by the Iranians. The Mughal Empire was now established.

Up until this time various cultures and religions were absorbed into what was evolving into the prevailing religion, the Hinduism of today. Islam was the exception to this syncretizing process. It maintained its distinction, which eventually led to the birth of Pakistan.

Influenced by the devotional emphasis of Hinduism and Sufi Islam, Nanak founded Sikhism (in Punjabi *sikh* means disciple) in Punjab, North-Western India. Guru Nanak (1469–1538 CE) as he came to be called, believed that God transcends religious distinctions.

It was an exhausted and weakened Mughal Empire that the British took advantage of in the eighteenth century. A Hindu diaspora disseminated itself at this time, with another major wave just after the Second World War, particularly to North America and Britain.

Chapter 3

Origins

The Vedic literature the Aryans brought with them into the Indian subcontinent is the authoritative basis for Hinduism. A central belief is in the existence of a cosmic or natural order – *rta*, a balanced way of living: physically, socially, ethically and spiritually. The language in which Vedic ideas were expressed reflected their original homelands, which had been much further north where sunlight and fire were greatly valued. Nature was considered of central importance: there is a strong ecological emphasis in Vedic teaching.

This oral tradition, the Veda, consisted primarily of collections of hymns, detached poetical portions and ceremonial formulas. Tradition has it that the Vedas are revealed *shruti* (heard) knowledge. The orthodox view regards them as divine revelation with no specific author, either human or divine.

Let us reflect for a moment on who these people were. Texts show their society was of high civilization and ethics. They seem to have initiated

⊙ *The cosmic sun*

the Iron Age and pursued science and technology. We do not as yet know exactly why they migrated from their native territory* but, when they did, they ensured their culture and knowledge were secured.

This is how it was done: a group of people memorized the main material syllable by syllable so that it was preserved orally. To maintain the integrity of the material different Brahmin families had responsibility for different parts of the material. They devised ingenious ways of preserving and

* Recent findings suggest that dwellers in the Black Sea region were forced to migrate by a great flood c. 5000 BCE.

⊙ Left to right: Lakshmana (Rama's brother), Rama, Sita (Rama's wife)
Bottom left: Rama's devotee, Hanuman, the monkey god

handing on their intellectual material. Several techniques were built in to ensure the precise assembly of the material, including a form of error correction rather like we use today on the Internet.

The Aryans were a virile pastoral people and their horse-drawn chariots and composite bows must have given them a great advantage in dominating much of Northern India. In turn, the local non-Aryan culture must also have exerted an influence. Ritual status was the important element and the varna orders became a mechanism for integrating the new ethnic groups. The local elite were absorbed into the varnas, depending on their own place in their society. A proportion of the subjugated non-Aryans seem to have become the fourth varna – the *Dasas* (servants) – and were referred to as the *Shudras*. As various conquering and other groups arrived they became subgroups within the system and were known as *jati* (meaning race, from *ja* – born or begotten, also *jar* – root). These have come to have a greater relevance for day-to-day working than the main varnas.

Although some of the numerous tribes became assimilated into the main groups, many retained their own identity. Eventually, an underclass – those who had been cast out – emerged. They grouped together as 'untouchables': they did all the dirty jobs. Even today the price paid for doing

something unforgivable in villages in India is a form
of social ostracism. Essentially, no one will smoke
or share water with you.

Today, the descendants of the 'untouchables'
comprise roughly 15 per cent of the population.
Eventually, in an effort to raise their status,
Mahatma Gandhi gave them the name of *harijan* –
God's people. The politically correct term for these
groups is 'scheduled castes', although they prefer
to call themselves *dalits* (the oppressed).

Social Hierarchy

Society began to evolve vertically in hereditary
groups with a definite Aryan ascendancy. This
stratification was maintained by alliances in the form
of intermarriage within a few families. The resulting
biological columns have continued for several centuries. These groupings were often economically
based, and the advantaged were referred to as
'belonging to such and such clan with two or three
houses'. The system evolved over the centuries and
became a powerful way of ordering society.

The priests were the 'spin doctors' of their day.
They were not slow to realize the significance of
maintaining a hierarchy, with the supreme
authority vested in the highest group. Priests
managed to secure and keep the first position by

claiming that only they could bestow divinity on the king. They increased their power base by assimilating local legendary heroes and gods into the pantheon, sometimes attributing their deeds to one of the major Vedic gods.

Varnas: A Culture of Inequality

The first three varnas are considered *dvija* (twice born), once through physical birth and then through the initiation of the young males in Vedic rituals. From the aspect of social organization the most striking characteristic of Hindu culture is the extreme emphasis placed on inequality of status, which underlies the system of the varnas. Almost a third of the 'Hindu' population of India is barred from normal (Brahmanic) Hindu practices. The shudras, dalits and the various tribal groups practise their own brand of Hinduism, with certain common features. Quite a large number have converted to Buddhism and Christianity.

Inevitably, the Brahmins became the ultimate authority and gave spiritual guidance. Everything was prescribed and worked out, everyone knew their place and were told what they must do in any given situation. This became known as the Brahmanical period and through the ages legends were created to support the prevailing politics. A later Vedic hymn* even provides

* *Rig-Veda* 10, 90, 12.

an account of the mythical origins of the varnas: 'The Brahmins issued from the mouth of the god Brahma (the first of the triad of gods) at the moment of creation, of his arms were made the Kshatriya, his thighs became the Vaishya, of his feet the Shudra was born.'

» Who Can Be A Hindu?

Hinduism has an extraordinary ability to absorb foreign elements, which has contributed to the religion's syncretism – the wide variety of beliefs and practices that it encompasses. It sees itself as a universal religion because of its profound influence on various other faiths during its long, unbroken history. However, the ultra-orthodox believe that to be Hindu both parents must be Hindus born in India. The following table illustrates a simplified viewpoint:

H0 The core group consists of all those Brahmins, Kshatriyas and Vaishyas who were born in India, either before or after partition from Pakistan, and whose ancestors were Hindus.

H1 Those who have either both parents or father belonging to any of the three varnas, who either live overseas or have travelled overseas. They need to undergo ritual purification before being allowed to participate in various religious ceremonies.

H2 The Shudras – although barred from orthodox practices, they are part of the varna classification.

H3 Harijans and some tribal groups.

H4 Christians, Sikhs, Buddhists, Jains, all those who believe in their concept of God.

It is debatable into which category 'converts' to Hinduism fit, as traditionally you have to be born a Hindu. This would include those who have joined sects like the Hari Krishna movement and non-Hindu males who have married into any of the three varnas, and their children. This group and H4 would paradoxically be allowed into many of the temples which are closed to H2 and H3.

Jnana Yoga

With the advent of Buddhism and in response to Islam, the Vedic culture that had taken root was beginning to decline. By the eighth century, Vedic teaching appeared less important, and it was perceived that the purity of the Vedas was being lost.

Hinduism received its greatest impetus from Shankara (788–820 CE), who is often described as one of Hinduism's most eminent philosophers. His philosophical system is in the tradition of *Advaita Vedanta,* non-dualism, in *jnana* (knowledge) yoga development. It is based on an unequivocal belief in the authority of the Vedas. He founded the *Dasanami* (ten names or branches) order of *sannyasis* (those who have renounced worldly things – similar to monks). This order still exists and has four centres of learning: Dwarka in the west, Puri in the east, Badri in the north and

Shringeri in the south. The heads of these centres
each hold the title of Shankaracharya (*acharya* =
spiritual guide).

Bhakti Yoga

Two other developments took place at about the
same time as Shankara. There had been a gradual
shift from the ritual to a personal relationship with
God. This second group received its impetus from
the Tamil *bhakti* (devotional) cults in South India.
A Tamil Brahmin, Ramanuja, disagreed with
Shankaracharaya's theory that knowledge was the
primary means of salvation. According to him it
was merely one of the means and not nearly as
effective as devotion, giving oneself up entirely to
God. Ramanuja was an effective bridge between
the devotional cults and Hindu theology, as was
Madhva, another South Indian.

Many devotional songs came to be written in
both North and South India and, although there
were some Brahmins among the writers, the
majority of the preachers were from the lower
jatis, notably Kabir, a low-jati weaver who
preached Hindu and Muslim unity, and Tukaram,
a Maharashtrian Shudra. Women such as Mirabai,
a princess of Rajasthan, also contributed to the
bhakti movement.

Karma Yoga

The Nath Sampradaya (*nath* – protector, *sampra-daya* – tradition) is a good example of the third type of development: *karma* (action) yoga. This group is particularly noteworthy as participation was open to anyone regardless of religion, gender or social class. Great value was placed on the improvement of environmental conditions and the establishment of a solid economic infrastructure. Education was encouraged and provided for all who could take advantage of it. The Nath Sampradaya had a high regard for science and medicine: many of their leading figures were accomplished scientists and researchers. They were seen as a direct challenge to orthodox Hinduism.

Its most important founder, Goraksha (*go* – light or rays, + *raksha* – to protect) was originally a Buddhist. He and his followers Hinduized Buddhist *Tantras,* producing a synthesis of Shaivism (Shaivas are followers of Shiva, one of the Hindu triad of gods) and Buddhism. Tantra is a deeply ecological term that roughly translates as 'web'. It signifies a mutually interdependent phenomenal world woven by the complex interplay of order and chaos. Nathism became popular and travelled to Nepal, Tibet and China.

⊙ *Left to right: Sarasvati, Lakshmi and Ganesha*

Whilst Goraksha is hardly known in the
West, he has had a profound influence. He
is the patron of Nepal and the Gurkhas take
their name from him. More than any other great
figure to emerge up to his time, Goraksha

advocated a holistic approach to life. The tradition is largely responsible for the development of the Hatha yoga practice of postures, breathing techniques and other psycho-spiritual exercises.

Chapter 4

Aims & Beliefs

For Hindus, Hinduism is more than just a religion. It is a way of life. Their own name for Hinduism is Sanatana Dharma (*Sanatana* – eternal, + *dharma* – order); it is distinguished from Brahmanism or Vedic Dharma.

Duty and Fulfilment

Sva-dharma (personal duty) is all important. The *Bhagavad Gita* (Song of God) makes it clear that it is better to do one's own duty (however poorly done) than someone else's (however well that is carried out).

The *Bhagavad Gita* is the Hindu's favourite religious text. It is a beautifully written spiritual poem and an integral part of the *Mahabharata* epic. It focuses on the importance of carrying out disinterested action in doing one's duty along the path of fulfilment. The emphasis is on duty rather than on asserting one's rights.

Although the Vedas are the ultimate canonical

⊙ *Bathing in the Ganges*

authority for all Hindus, their actual contents are unknown to most people. Hindus generally follow family traditions and accept the guidance provided by their priests without question.

Three Stages in Life

In the Brahmanical system there are three stages in life, known as *varnashrams* (*varna ashram* – stage, resting-place). The stages, applicable to the twice-

born, are: *brahamchari* – one who is a student;
grihastha – one who is a householder; *vanaprastha*
– one who has retired from active life. A fourth
stage, *sannyasi* – one who has renounced worldly
things, was added at a later point, presumably
influenced by Buddhism. These stages are
observed notionally by all, but in reality by only a
very few. The grihastha is the most important
socially as the householder sustains the others.

❯ The Four Human Accomplishments

There are four *purushartha* (human accomplishments):
Artha acceptance of wealth, possession and power – the objects
of worldly activity, the creation of a sustainable society
Dharma cosmic order which is maintained by righteousness and
observing social and religious law
Kama achieving quality and enjoyment of life in a balanced
way, not to be confused with hedonism
Moksha the ultimate goal, liberation from the cycle of
births and deaths

For most Hindus, the quality of life is rated just as important as a
better birth. They generally believe that a correct balance of
the first three aims will eventually lead to moksha. The minority
that consider moksha the most important join one of the various
sects according to their personal needs and beliefs.

Three Obligations

Each individual is said to have three obligations:
- to the gods – addressed through daily worship, rituals and regular guidance provided by priests
- to the sages – achieved by the study of the Veda, the chanting of mantras and through offering hospitality to Brahmins
- to the ancestors – fulfilled by producing a son to perpetuate the family and necessary to perform the funeral rites for ancestors.

Death and Reincarnation

For Hindus, religion is not an alternative to the world: it is primarily the means of improving their existence in it. Hindus believe that the individual reincarnates under conditions created through the history of their own past behaviour. Each incarnation provides an opportunity to be born into a higher varna and better circumstances. This is only likely to occur if they have been *dharmic* (righteous). Righteousness is the result of doing one's own duty in the prescribed or proper manner.

Karma is an important concept in this context. It is synonymous with the consequences of any action – be they right or wrong. There is no concept of guilt or sin in the way it is commonly perceived in the West. Rather, the notion of karma is an understanding of the great loop of effects which returns to the instigator of an action. Everyone has to accept responsibility for their own actions.

Three Kinds of *Karma*

Karma is of three kinds. First, that which has begun to bear fruit in life. Little or nothing can be done about these current consequences. They have to be endured or enjoyed. Such karma may explain how sometimes villains unfairly appear to prosper whilst good people have problems.

Second, there is karma in the making, the effects of which will influence the future.

Third, there is karma that has accumulated but not been activated. It is possible to ameliorate or neutralize such latent consequences by timely action. There are various methodologies such as ritual prayers to achieve this.

The word *atma* is sometimes erroneously translated as 'soul'. Atma comes from a Rig-Vedic (one of the Vedas) term for 'breath'. This later developed into the notion of 'higher self' (*paramatma*), which is identical with Brahman – the Supreme, One without a second, the Singularity.

Traditionally, it is believed that the human personality is multi-layered. It is often conceived as composed of seven *koshas* (successive layers which include the physical organism, bioenergetic process and mental states). The physical organism is a complex standing wave of physical materials. Death (*mrita*) occurs when the bioenergetic processes no longer maintain the physical body. However, the embodied history (sometimes called *sanskaras* – memory construction) is retained. This leads to reincarnation again and again, to fulfil karmas and work through the cycle of consequences. Thus the great cycle of birth and death continues until the individual achieves moksha.

Chapter 5

Teachings & Doctrines

The majority of Hindus are satisfied with the teachings provided by the Brahmins and family traditions. Some literate Hindus make the reading of the *Bhagavad Gita* a part of their daily routine. Through the voice of Krishna, the *Bhagavad Gita* preaches three complementary paths: bhakti yoga (way of devotion), karma yoga (way of action) and jnana yoga (way of knowledge). Devotion is considered the most accessible path as it is open to ordinary people – women and Shudras alike.

For most Hindus the paths of devotion and action take the form of everyday rituals, visits to temples and occasional pilgrimages. The path of knowledge commonly takes the form of *satsang* (the company of the good and the great). In practical terms it means congregating to listen to spiritual leaders, or participation in activities such as the reading of sacred texts. Intellectual stimulation is provided by lectures and discourses given by proponents of any of the orthodox systems of thought described below.

There is a small minority who wish to do more

⊗ *The mark of Shiva*

than know about truth and seek to realize truth in
life. For this group teachings are contained in the
intellectual heritage of the *darshana* (perspectives,
philosophical insight).

Sankhya

The foundation of all orthodox doctrines is the
Veda. From this, one of the oldest known systems
of philosophy was developed. Called the *Sankhya*,
it is said to have been founded by the legendary
genius Kapila. We must quickly rescue this term
from some Western scholars and others who

mistake and restrict Sankhya to the work of a late student of the Ishvarakrishna philosophy.

The term Sankhya is derived from the idea of categorizing and enumerating both phenomenal and transcendental experience. According to Sankhya philosophy, objective and subjective realism and idealism are neither alternatives nor opposites. They are two complementary aspects of one ultimate reality, which transcends them.

Kapila's Sankhya identifies and enumerates 26 schools of Sankhya which can be distinguished by the number of fundamental categories that they admit (24, 25 or 26). Each system is essentially similar at the phenomenal level. All phenomena are composed of *gunas* (quality/string), three substantial qualities (*triguna*) that emerge from an unmanifest, transcendental state (*prakriti* – concept of nature). These qualities are never found in isolation but always in relative combination. Such combinations give rise to the entire universe of phenomena. They are *tamas* (potentiality), *sattva* (actuality) and *rajas* (activity). There are no English equivalents to these three Sanskrit words, so they are translated into different terms depending on their context. Understanding the meaning of the *triguna* is a necessary key to Hinduism.

At the root of the tree of Sankhya is Brahman, already described as a Singularity. It has no

❱❱ The Tree of Sankhya

BRAHMAN (equivalent to Ishvara [god] in theistic version) 26

PURUSHA (transcendental subject, consciousness) 25

PRAKRITI (transcendental object, nature) 24

MAHAT (also called Buddhi, intelligence = the choice-maker) 23

AHAMKARA (the self/world producer) 22

MANAS (mind consciousness) 21

TANMATRAS (sensations/affordance)

shabda (sound) 10	*rasa* (flavour) 4
sparsha (touch) 8	*gandha* (odour) 2
rupa (appearance) 6	

JNANENDRIYAS (cognitive capacities)

chaksura (sight) 20	*rasa* (taste) 17
shravana (hearing) 19	*sparsha* (touch) 16
ghrana (smell) 18	

KARMENDRIYAS (conative [effort] capacities)

hasta (manipulation) 15	*pay* (excretion) 12
pada (ambulation) 14	*upastha* (pro/re-creation) 11
vacha (communication) 13	

MAHABHUTAS (great elements)

akasha (ether) 9	*apas* (liquids) 3
vayu (gases) 7	*prithvi* (solids) 1
teja (plasma) 5	

describable qualities and is beyond space and time. Some later thinkers were unable to justify the idea as it transcends discursive argument (26 element version) and their versions of Sankhya do not include it (25 element version). Others went further and dropped the notion of *purusha*. This is roughly the concept of a subjective transcendental self and is contrasted with *prakriti*, which is a concept of transcendental nature. Still other versions of Sankhya hold that purusha and prakriti are both aspects of nature (24 element version).

At the phenomenal level, Sankhya distinguishes an intelligent principle called *mahat* or *buddhi*. *Ahamkara* (the self-maker) is the means by which different phenomenal selves are enacted together with their complementary worlds. The integrated realm of *manas* (mental experience) is further divided into five perspectives, each of which are enumerated in terms of their efferent (outward), afferent (inward), ontological (nature of being) and aesthetic categories. Phenomenologically, we act and respond to a world of things which afford various sensations.

Six Orthodox Systems

All six orthodox systems of Hindu philosophy tacitly assume and accept the Vedic doctrine or they would de facto reject the authority of the Veda and thereby be rejected as heterodox. These are: the *Sankhya* of Ishvarakrishna, the *Nyaya* of Gautama, *Vaisheshika* of Kanada, *Yoga* of Patanjali, *Mimamsa* of Jaimini and *Vedanta* of Badarayana, to which might be added the contributions of Ramanuja and Shankaracharya. Buddhist philosophy, which rejects the ultimate authority of the Veda, is therefore not considered orthodox.

Ishvarakrishna

The best known Sankhya exposition in the West is that of Ishvarakrishna and his classic treatise the *Sankhya Karika*. Ishvarakrishna was unable to justify the existence of Brahman on a logical basis but certainly did not deny the existence of God. If he had, it would have been contrary to the Veda.

Nyaya and *Vaisheshika*

Both *Nyaya* (analysis) and *Vaisheshika* (specific characteristics) are highly analytical systems. The Naiyayikas (those who follow the *Nyaya* tradition) regard the *Nyaya Sutras* (*sutra* – string, i.e. string of axioms and rules) of Gautama as the primary source of their system. Gautama was from another branch of Gautama the Buddha's family, around the beginning of the Common Era. Nyaya deals mainly with logic and stresses epistemological (theory of knowledge) issues and procedures. The

Vaisheshika Sutras were probably produced a century or so earlier and emphasize ontological issues – the nature and relations of being.

Yoga Sankhya

Yoga (union, oneness) *Sankhya* is a philosophy ascribed to Patanjali and expounded as his *Yoga Sutras*. He believed that a system of graduated practices lead to higher stages and ultimately to *kaivalyam* (liberation). This is described as *ashtanga* (eight limbs) yoga (not to be confused with the Hatha Yoga system described above).

Mimamsa

Mimamsa (inquiry) is a system is divided into two distinct branches: *purva* – prior, chiefly concerned with the correct interpretation of Vedic rituals; and *uttara* – the later school. This system is mainly concerned with discussing the nature of Brahman, the ultimate reality. Eventually, the school merged with Vedanta.

Vedanta

Vedanta (*Veda* + *anta* – end/culmination of the Vedas). The philosophical concepts contained in the Upanishads (see pages 101–103) served as the basis for Vedanta. The Vedantins emerged as the most important interpreters of Hindu philosophy around 700 CE and remain so to this day. The central

The Eight *Angas* (Limbs)

YAMA – observance of:

   satya – truth

   ahimsa – non-violence

   asteya – non-stealing

   aparigraha – non-grasping

   brahmacharya – study of the absolute, sexual restraint, usually the period of being a student

NIYAMA – practice of:

   saucha – purity

   tapasya – observing one's own actions

   santosha – contentment

   svadhyaya – study of physics and metaphysics

   isvarpranidhani – identification with Ishvara

ASANA – poise, both mental and physical

PRANAYAMA – expansion of the life-force

PRATYAHARA – sense withdrawal

DHARANA – fixation of attention

DHYANA – total concentration state of pure awareness

SAMADHI – complete absorption

message is that the goal of the Vedas is not the performance of ritual. Rather, it is the achievement of understanding of the truth to which the ritual points and one's commitment to it.

Chapter 6

Practices

Human needs have both a mental and a social manifestation. The social expression of needs is very much influenced by culture. Everyday practices in Hinduism have evolved in an effort to cater for these needs and to provide a framework for every stage in life. The ethos is one of timelessness but timing is all-important, whether it is the opening of a new shop or setting the date of a wedding. Working out these times astrologically is the function of the priests who use the Hindu calendar. They also prescribe the format events should adopt, guiding people through the various stages of successful performance.

The Brahmanic Time-Scale

Traditionally, the duration of one universe (and there are many) on the relative time-scale equals the life-span of its ruler Brahma. He lives a hundred Brahmanic years, which represent 311,040,000 million human years. A *kalpa* (one day of Brahma) represents only one cycle in the life of

⊙ *Priest applying the* bindi *to the forehead on a visit to the temple*

the universe, equal to 4,320 million years; this is
followed by Brahma's night, a period of rest when
everything is in suspension. Dissolution occurs
and the period when everything is reabsorbed into
the divine source is known as Brahma's death, or
the great night. The cycle starts again with the
birth of the new Brahma.

The kalpa is divided into 1,000 *mahayugas*
(*maha* – great, + *yuga* – ages); each of these lasts
4,320,000 years and is further divided into four
yugas, each accompanied by a progressive decline

of *dharma* (righteousness). The four yugas are: the *Satyayuga* (also called *Kritayuga*) – a time of high moral order, the golden age (1,728,000 years), represented by the sacred cow of dharma, who is balanced firmly on four legs; *Tretayuga* – (1,296,000 years), when dharma is more or less steady on three legs; *Dvaparayuga* – when dharma balances on two legs for 864,000 years; and *Kaliyuga*, the present age (432,000 years), when righteousness is imagined teetering on one leg.

The Hindu Calendar

Although the Gregorian Calendar may have been adopted for secular purposes, the Hindu calendar is used for all religious purposes. According to this calendar a 2,000-year period was completed in April 1944 and a new millennium began.

Lunar Months

Based on solar reckoning the lunar year consists of approximately 360 days divided into twelve lunar months. Periodic adjustments to align it with the solar year are made by inserting an extra month. This month is considered impure and ceremonies such as weddings do not take place during this time. Nor are weddings celebrated from August through to

❯❯ Structure of the Hindu Calendar

There are twelve months, divided into six *ritu* (seasons).

SEASONS

Vasanta – spring

Grishma – summer

Varsha – rains/monsoons

Sharad – autumn

Hemanta – winter

Shishira – frosty

MONTHS

Chaitra – March/April

Vaisakha – April/May

Jaishtha – May/June

Asadha – June/July

Sravana – July/August

Bhadrapada – August/September

Asvina – September/October

Karttika – October/November

Margashirsha – November/December

Pausa – December/January

Magha – January/February

Phalguna – February/March

October, although certain rituals connected with the fulfilment of desires are allowed.

The month is counted from full moon to full moon. It is divided into two, the dark half (when the moon is waning) and the light half (when the moon is waxing). Special rituals are prescribed on the days of the new moon and full moon, such as certain fasts.

Festivals provide a definite social structure to the year and are specific to the various groups and sects. However, Diwali and Holi (see Myths) are celebrated by the whole of the Hindu community.

Diwali

Diwali (from *Dipavali* – lights), celebrated during Karttika, welcomes Lakshmi, the goddess of wealth, into the home, which is decorated with small oil lamps and candles. There are displays of fireworks, much feasting and exchange of presents such as clothes and jewellery.

Holi

Holi is held on the last full moon day of Phalguna in the spring. Members of all classes (and often from other religions) and sexes mingle, sprinkling one another with cascades of coloured powders and liquids. It is a day when grievances are forgotten, people embrace each other and get together to eat, drink, sing and dance.

Other Festivals

Other festivals include Vasantpanchami, celebrated in Magha (January/February) and dedicated to the goddess Sarasvati, who is honoured with music and dance performances; Dussehra is celebrated on the tenth day of Asvina. Other, regionally specific festivals include Pongal in Tamil-speaking areas, Durga-puja in Bengal and Ganesha Chaturtha in Maharashtra.

Raksha Bandhan

Festivals need not always be dedicated to a god or goddess, for example the festival of *raksha* (protection) + *bandhan* (to tie), which is held in the month of Sravana (July/August). This delightful festival is mainly celebrated in North India. Girls and married women tie a *rakhi* – made from a twisted gold or yellow and red thread – on the right wrist of their brother and feed him with Indian sweetmeats. For his part, he promises to protect his sister and gives her a gift in return. Sometimes the gesture is extended to a brother-in-law; if the brother happens to be abroad, the rakhi arrives by post.

There are different stories about the origins of Raksha Bandhan. But one charming version relates how the Hindu queen Padmini sought protection from the Mughal Emperor by sending him a rakhi after she was threatened by a minor Muslim king. The Emperor respected the rakhi and defended the honour of Padmini. In the same way, even today, in

⌃ The Festival of Holi. (Courtesy Victoria and Albert Museum)

India and in Hindu communities all over the world a rakhi is usually honoured, even when the recipient is not a Hindu.

Food and Pollution

Traditionally, the importance of a good diet, its effects on the body and the hygiene requirements for proper preparation are well accepted, although interpreted ritualistically. According to Manu (there are many Manus – the first human being, an ancient law-giver and the founding fathers of humankind), 'a healthy diet produces a healthy body and a healthy body produces a healthy mind'.

Food is categorized according to its effects. These are described as three *gunas** (properties). First, **sattvic foods,** which are generally light and nutritious. This group consists of dairy products, and some legumes, cereals, fruits and vegetables, but little or no spices. **Rajasic foods** are those that cause heat and stimulation in the body. They include the same food groups, although the difference lies mainly in the liberal use of spices and herbs in their preparation. The third kind of foods, the **tamasic** group, also includes fish and meat. Such food is euphem- istically called 'tasty'

* As pointed out earlier, if is believed that all phenomena are composed of gunas. For example, these properties can be applied to food as here, or people.

and is characterized by hot, spicy, bitter and fermented foods, which have a dulling effect. Stale or foods past their use-by date are considered tamasic.

Specific foods are chosen and prepared for different occasions. Generally, there are two ways of preparing food: *pukka* (deep fried) and *katcha* (raw, including boiled, lightly fried and baked food dishes). It is permitted to accept pukka foods from a class lower than your own, but not katcha. Thus, an orthodox family which is travelling can eat deep fried foods with impunity. Mostly, food that has come into contact with another person, even accidentally, is unacceptable. The cook must not taste the food after cooking as that would make it impure. All food must be offered to the gods before it is consumed.

Vegetarianism is not universal among Hindus. The diet of the Vedic Aryans, which included fish, meat, cereals, fruits, vegetables, dairy products and liquor, is still enjoyed by many. Traditional families, particularly Brahmins, prefer to remain vegetarian and will avoid onion, garlic and alcohol. Food prepared for use in temples must not be polluted by these ingredients. In certain sects, notably the Tantric, meat, fish and alcohol are partaken in a ritual form. Certain Brahmin families in the south and coastal regions will eat fish but not meat. Even in families where meat is eaten, quite often the women of the house are vegetarians. All Hindus generally avoid beef as the cow is considered sacred.

Fasting

Fasting is generally considered a religious act and is voluntary. Most people, apart from sannyasis and other ascetics, undertake fasts chiefly to achieve some purpose or material object. There are a variety of fasts, which do not always means going without food. They are undertaken with different objectives and formats. Some involve going without water; for others fasting means avoiding salt and eating only fruit, sweet things or special preparations such as those made with nuts or specific cereals.

There are weekly and annual fasts. A fast may be kept on a particular day of the week dedicated to one's chosen deity, although this is not universal. Saturday is considered Hanuman's day but then so is Tuesday. He is extremely popular with wrestlers. Monday fasts are dedicated to Shiva – by young girls to obtain a husband like Shiva, and married women for the longevity of their husband's lives.

Currently, one of the most popular fasts is the one dedicated to Santoshi Mata (Mother of Contentment – see Modern Movements) and observed every Friday. She is very popular with women, who point out that she does not desire material gifts, only the affection of her devotees. Unlike other deities she is good at granting material boons like cars, televisions and a husband's promotion. Annual fasts include those dedicated to Shiva and Krishna on their traditional birthdays.

Role of Women

Traditionally, a married woman is considered a *sahadharmi* (the husband's partner – albeit a junior one, in dharma), and it is as a unit that they perform rituals. Women play an important role, although they are not considered, by the highly orthodox, sufficiently worthy to study the Vedas. They are idealized in sacred and other literature, where there are references to female philosophers and teachers.

Daughters are regarded as 'wealth belonging to another family' as ultimately they are given away in marriage. The birth of a daughter, particularly the second or third, is considered a burden because of the insidious dowry system. For about a thousand years now only basic education (if at all) has been made available to most women. They are usually married whilst in their early teens to men five to ten years older.

It is considered a curse to be childless and almost always the woman is held responsible. Inevitably, women will go to great lengths to produce a child, preferably a son. There are many religious practices to bring this about, from magical potions and rituals to pilgrimages and visiting special holy men for their 'blessings'.

Hindu widows of the 'twice-born' *dvija* group are not expected to remarry. They are marked out by their white clothes and live a life of piety and celibacy. They are often regarded as being harbingers of bad luck and are kept away from religious functions and ceremonies. Many of these practices were challenged by the religious reform movements, which actively encouraged the participation of women in a wider area of social activity. Changes have slowly begun to occur in the middle classes but the old traditions still continue in villages and amongst the lower classes.

Rites of passage relating to women include the purification after first menstruation for a young girl. Also, women are not allowed near the kitchen or in temples for the first three days of menstruation, and then, only after the ritual bath. Ritual purification also takes place after the birth of a child.

The oldest woman in the extended family system is of paramount importance. She reigns absolutely over the daughters-in-law. Almost everyone else, including the sons and grandsons, defer to her.

Cleanliness

Ritual purity is something of an obsession with members of the first three varnas. The orthodox *dvija* group consider themselves to be polluted if they come into contact with the lowest groups, who are considered unclean. Indeed, even today in India, a Brahmin priest must ritually bathe if as much as the shadow of a *dalit* falls on him.

The orthodox consider travelling overseas unclean and corrupting, thus there are elaborate cleansing rituals after returning home. These may include bathing in a sacred river such as the Ganges. A period of contamination lasts for thirteen days after the death of a blood relative and no affected adult is allowed to carry out normal duties such as cooking. Everyone must rinse their hands and mouth before prayers, after attending a funeral and before and after meals.

The five products of the sacred cow: milk, yoghurt, ghee (clarified butter), urine and faeces – are used in certain purifying rituals. The five products represent the five layers of phenomenal experience enumerated in Sankhya. The cow carries the crescent shape of the moon in the form of its horns and is a symbol of the mind (manas). The five products represent the five layers of phenomenal experience enumerated in Sankhya.

Chapter 7

Ritual & Worship

Worship is usually undertaken on an individual basis. Sometimes, however, a group in a temple or home might sing an *arti* hymn of invocation together. This is generally done after the arti ceremony, which consists of waving a lighted lamp in front of the *murti* (image of a deity) as an offering of light. Before worship, a small amount of water is taken in the palm of the right hand and sipped, invoking the name of Vishnu. This is a purification ritual and must be done three times. After worship in a temple it is traditional to walk once clockwise around the murti.

Sometimes, women will cover their head when they enter the temple. However, this is an individual preference and not a universal custom amongst Hindus. It is perceived as a mark of respect, just as women in certain families will cover their head in the presence of their father-in-law. Before entering the temple it is customary to remove the shoes and leave them outside the temple, together with other items made of leather.

⊙ *Decorating the floor with a* rangoli *pattern*

In temples as well as homes the murti has to be
installed with due ceremony by a priest. The murtis
might be made of marble, stone, brass, copper or
clay, occasionally gold or silver (if they are in the
private shrine of a rich industrialist). The deity is
believed to take up residence in the murti during
the consecration ceremony. From then, it must
never be left on its own. It must be looked after and
worshipped day and night, and even more often if it
is in a temple. In addition to making offerings, the
puja (worship) takes the form of bathing, clothing

and decorating the murti. Any food prepared is first offered to the gods and then distributed as *prasada* (grace) to everyone present.

Three Kinds of Ritual

There are three kinds of ritual: *nitya* (essential and regular); *naimittika* (occasional); and *kamya* (voluntary and intentional).

Nitya

Nitya rituals are practised every day in homes as well as in temples. Most homes have a small shrine or separate room where the deity is installed. In temples the duties are carried out by special, designated priests at different times of the day. In families, particularly extended families, the senior member (generally the female), takes charge of them. If for any reason the whole family has to travel away from home, someone is invited to remain to look after the deities. In extreme circumstances the murtis may be carried to another home or a temple and installed with due ceremony.

Depending on personal preferences, offerings may also be made to *Surya* (the sun) and the sacred *tulsi* (basil) plant. Milk is offered to local snakes, sacred trees and obscure spirits (benevolent and malevolent) dwelling in the garden or at cross-roads or other sacred places in the community. Puja is also done before starting work, be it in a factory, shop, or in a taxi or bus.

Naimittika

Naimittika rituals include all rites of passage (*sanskaras*). These begin with birth and the first time the child eats solid food. Later rites include the first haircut, particularly for young boys. Prayers are offered to Sarasvati, the goddess of learning, before children go to school for the first time.

The *yajnapavita* (*yajna* – fire ritual, + *pavita* – purify) procedure is sometimes called the sacred thread ceremony. It is regarded as crucial for permitted boys in their early teens. This is the second spiritual birth. After various purification rites the young man is invested with a sacred thread (symbolizing continuity, the cycle of birth and death). The gods are asked to dwell in and strengthen him. The *Gayatri* mantra is repeated into his right ear, giving him the right to utter it and study the Vedas. The Gayatri mantra from the *Rig-Veda* (3, 62, 10) is one of the most sacred and symbolic of the texts, alhough few today know its meaning (see overleaf).

» *Gayatri* Mantra

(*om bhur bhuvahh svah*)
tat savitur varenyam
bhargo devasya dhimahi
dhiyo yo nah prachodayat

Interpretation (*om* material realm, bioenergetic realm, cognitive realm)
'Let us concentrate on attaining fulfilment and strive for the dawning
of the highest consciousness.'

The words in parentheses are traditionally
added before reciting the Gayatri. Many Hindus
recite the Gayatri 108 times as part of their daily
prayers. A rosary string of 108 beads of various
materials may be used to keep count. Rosaries
made from *rudraksha* (tears of Shiva), a kind of
berry, are most prized for this purpose.

A personal guru may give an individual mantra
to a disciple with specific instructions on how,
when, where and the number of times to chant.
This practice has spread widely via the
Transcendental Meditation movement.

Kamya

Pilgrimages fall into the kamya category, including
those undertaken to achieve some benefit, such as
the birth of a son. It is widely believed that moksha
will be attained by taking elderly parents to the four
main shrines of Vishnu in the course of one year.

These sites are hundreds of miles apart and the journey takes considerable organization.

The *yajna* ceremony is often translated as a sacrificial ritual. The origins are in early Vedic times when, for instance, a cow or horse might be sacrificed amidst an elaborate ceremony. It was a special and grand affair not undertaken lightly. The practice and ideology of the yajnas are of two kinds: a public one conducted by several priests and the much simpler domestic ritual.

In both forms of the ritual, ghee and herbs are offered (thrown in) to a specially lit fire accompanied by specific Vedic chants. This is a central part of most ceremonies, especially those connected with the rites of passage, but it should not be confused with the sacrificial slaughter of animals or birds, which is a rare practice today, followed only by certain sects and tribes. A vital part of completing any ritual is the offering of *dakshina** (a kind of levy or fee) to the priest. The size of the dakshina is commensurate with the importance of the occasion.

Rites of Passage

Marriage is one of the most important rites of passage for all four varnas. In the days before mass immigration into cities, marriages were arranged

* The word comes from *daksh* – the Sanskrit word for righteousness, which gives us an idea of its importance.

amongst people who knew each other or through the offices of the local barber or priest. Now, amongst the middle classes, marriages are arranged through the medium of classified advertisements in the Sunday newspapers. Advertisements are arranged to reflect the different varnas and jatis as relatively few inter-religious or inter-group marriages take place.

A short-list of candidates is prepared by a relative and then checked by the family priest for astrological and other forms of suitability with due regard to the horoscope. From this selection, the horoscopes of both the prospective bride and groom are matched. If they are suitable, the more progressive families arrange a chaperoned meeting between the young couple before the final choice is made. Although illegal in India, dowry negotiations are more often than not a part of the process: the family of the prospective groom has the upper hand. The astrological calendar is consulted again to choose a suitable date for the wedding. Marriages are performed according to Vedic ritual, although each jati has it own special customs.

After pregnancy is confirmed, blessings are given, usually by a priest, to produce a male child, ensure a successful delivery and the child's survival through the first six dangerous days after birth.

Last, but certainly not least, are the funeral ceremonies. The purpose of this last sanskara is to purify and console both the individual who has died and the bereaved. Hindus are generally cremated on open wooden pyres. In much of India, however, the rising cost of wood has promoted the use of electric crematoriums. The size of the pyre, and number of priests in attendance, depends on the social status of the family. The ashes are collected and after thirteen days sprinkled into a holy river such as the Ganges or into the ocean.

The first *shraddha* (paying respect to ones ancestors) ceremony is an important part of the funeral. The ceremony includes a symbolic offering of water and rice cakes. Thereafter, it is an annual commemoration. The first anniversary is considered to be the most important. This is partly because of the belief that it takes Yama (the god of death) a year to mete out the consequences of the individual's karma.

Chapter 8

Priesthood & Laity

According to Manu the person of a Brahmin is sacred; Brahmins are chief among all created beings; and other mortals enjoy life because of them. The Brahmin alone may interpret the sacred texts, the Vedas. The primary duties of the Brahmins are the study and teaching of the Veda, the performance of religious ceremonies for themselves and others, and the giving of spiritual guidance to others, who have to rely on them to gain the favour of the gods.

Although everyday religious practices incorporate many customs absorbed from other cultures, the most significant ceremonies are always Vedic. As such, these can be performed only by specialist Brahmin priests. Not all Brahmins, of course, are priests.

⊙ *Hindu priest*

» Priests with Special Training in the *Vedas*

Hotri specializes in reciting the *Rig-Veda*, which dates from the oldest Vedic period

Adhvaryu (also known as *Yajurvan*) is versed in the practical techniques of the *Yajur-Veda*

Udgataur chants the verses of the *Sama-Veda*

Atharvan specializes in the *Atharva-Veda*

Maharitvij great priest – supervises the above four chief priests

Ritvij priest who performs sacrificial ceremonies regularly

» Priests Who Perform Rituals

Purohit usually appointed as domestic chaplain in a royal family. Can also be attached to one or several families to conduct all the religious ceremonies. Often maintains the family records

Jangama different groups can have their own priests. This type pertains to the Lingayat Sect, a Shaiva movement in South India

Mahant head of a sect or group, e.g. Gorakshanath Math

Pujari those who officiate in temples

Mahapatras those who specialize in death rites

Other Priestly Functions

Certain common Brahmin family names describe the number of Vedas they had mastered. For example: mastery of two Vedas – *Divedi*, *Trivedi* (three) and *Chaturvedi* (four). *Agnihotri* – a *hotari* (officiating priest) who specializes in the *agni* (fire) rituals. *Agnihotara* is a fire offering.

In holy cities like Varanasi, there are *pandas* – priests – who meet pilgrims at the railway and bus stations and arrange accomodation for them. For many pilgrims the panda will belong to the same Brahmin family who has cared for them for generations. There are also *karmakandiyas* – priests who assist in specific rites, and *ghatias* – priests of a lower class with proprietary rights along the *ghats* (steps leading into the river) to tend to the needs of the ritual bathers.

Other familiar titles for teachers, generally Brahmins, are *guru*, *swami*, *acharya*, *rishi* and *maharishi*, *pundit*, *bhagwan*, *sant* and *baba*. Female teachers are known as *ma* or *mata* – mother, or *kumari* – virgin, goddess or heavenly being.

The *Sadhu* (Holy Man) Tradition

In India one often comes across *sadhus*. A sadhu is a good/ holy man, a religious mendicant; the female name is *sadhvi*. These are people who have chosen to live their life alone on the edges of society, or they may attach themselves to a group, order or temple. Owning neither personal nor community property they wear ochre robes and sometimes green, white or black ones. Certain groups remain naked, as in the *naga* (serpent) sadhu tradition, cover themselves with sacred ash and generally have long, matted hair. Some groups may have clean-shaven heads or occasionally a small tuft of hair will be left at the back.

Chapter 9

Holy Places & Sacred Sites

Early Vedic religion did not make use of temples. The place, usually outdoors, where the *yajgna* (ritual) was held became temporarily sacred. This practice still prevails for rituals carried out for the rites of passage. These are usually celebrated at home and a special square area is set aside in the garden or courtyard. Apartment-dwellers make use of public parks or gardens. The period during which the yajgna is held is also considered sacred. The benefits of participation by the *yajmana* (the patron of the ritual) result in developing a higher consciousness.

Where Temples Are Found

Temples are generally to be found in prominent, elevated positions, often with long flights of a specific number of steps. The ascent itself is a feature of the approach and signifies life's spiritual pilgrimage. Although the architectural style may vary, the construction of a temple itself has to

⊙ *Hindu shrine*

follow strict rules laid down in the *Puranas* (meaning 'old', 'stories of', traditional texts).

The Shri Swaminarayan Mandir (*mandir* – temple) at Neasden, London, is the largest temple outside India that has been built according to 'traditional rules'.

All temples must have an inner sanctuary where the images are installed. It is called the *garbhagrha* (womb house). Only the *dvija* (twice-born) are allowed to enter the inner sanctum. Several such important temples were built in caves, like those at Badrinath and Elephanta near Bombay.

Hindus currently talk about 'prayer halls', which can be found attached to many of the new temples. These halls are a new development and are generally used for educational purposes. Some of the older temples in India and elsewhere have large spaces in the form of a hall or a courtyard, whilst other temples are tiny one-chamber buildings.

Vishnu Temples

Special temples dedicated to Vishnu include those at Badrinath in the Himalayan foothills in Uttar Pradesh; Jagannath in Puri; Orissa; Dwarknath in Gujarat; and Triputhinath in the South. These are considered particularly sacred and are important places of pilgrimages. There are a number of Lakshmi-Narayan temples and others are dedicated to the important incarnations of Vishnu.

Angkor Wat in central Cambodia, built 1112–15 CE, is dedicated to Vishnu. It is thought to be the largest Hindu temple in the world, rising as high as 60 metres (200 feet). It is built entirely of stone, with relief friezes depicting scenes from Hindu mythology. The moat surrounding the temple complex is almost 4 km (2.5 miles) in circumference.

Shiva Temples

Temples devoted to Shiva (in phallic form) include
Amarnath in Kashmir; Kedarnath in the Himalayan
foothills in Uttar Pradesh; the Vishveshar temple in
Varanasi; Somnath in Gujarat; and Nasik in Mahar-
ashtra. In the temple in Chidambaram, Tamil Nadu,
Shiva is worshipped as Nataraj.

Kali Temples

Although there are temples devoted to various
goddesses all over India, the majority of them are
dedicated to Shiva's wife Sati in her various forms.
She is worshipped as Kali in Kalighat near Calcutta.
The actual temple was rebuilt in 1809 on a much
older site, where one of Sati's fingers is supposed
to have fallen (see Chapter 11 on Myths). Goats are
sacrificed there either as a thanksgiving or to ward
off a problem. Another well-known temple devoted
to Kali is in Kamakhya in Assam in Eastern India.
Sati's sexual parts fell here and it is a major centre
for Tantric ritual.

Brahma Temples

Whereas there are thousands of temples, only two
major temples are dedicated to Brahma. One is in
Khedbrahma and the other in Pushkar near Ajmer
in Rajasthan. There is also a lake near Pushkar

which like Lake Manasa in the Himalayas is believed to have healing properties.

Every village, town and city has temples dedicated to the various personal gods and their vehicles, generally animals or birds. A well- known temple is that of Karni Devi (another incarnation of Parvati), near Bikaner in Rajasthan. Because her vehicle, a rat, is venerated, rats are allowed to multiply freely and consequently there are hundreds occupying the temple andits grounds. Ganesha is particularly honoured in Maharashtra.

» The Seven Holy Cities

Ayodhya – believed to be the birthplace of Prince Rama, the hero of the *Ramayana*, and the ancient capital of his kingdom

Mathura – birthplace of Krishna

Haridwara – where the Ganges descends from the mountains onto the plains of North India

Gaya – sacred to Vishnu and also where Buddha achieved enlightenment

Varanasi (Kashi) – sacred to Shiva

Prayaga (Allahabad*) – in Uttar Pradesh

Dwarka**– the legendary capital of Krishna's kingdom

---

* This city was renamed the 'Abode of Allah' by his followers; the name is a source of friction amongst orthodox Hindus.
** It is suggested that the submerged ruins recently found off the coast of Gujarat may be Dwarka.

Sacred Rivers and Other Things in Nature

The seven sacred rivers are: Ganga (Ganges), Yamuna, Sarasvati (Sarasvati is not to be found on modern maps but is considered to be underground. It forms a triple confluence at Prayaga with the first two), Sindhu (Indus), Narmada, Godavari and Kaveri. The most revered of these is the Ganges. Millions of Hindus bathe in the Ganges every year to 'earn' good karma. Hindus all over the world will keep a little Ganges water in the house to perform the last rites. Bathing in the sea is valued but is not in the same class as bathing in the Ganges.

The conch shell is sacred and is often sounded before commencing rituals and worship. The banyan, *pippal* (a variety of ficus) and mango trees are considered holy. The leaves of the mango tree are hung around doors and windows for important ceremonies such as weddings. The wedding canopy is usually made up of whole banana plants. Basil leaves, marigold flowers and whole coconuts are important ingredients of rituals.

Sometimes flowers are presented in the form of a garland. Garlands are part of Indian culture and not special to Hindus; they are generally used to honour guests. A priest' however, would never be seen garlanding a woman, no matter how important she might be, because he might be seen as getting married to her. The exchange of garlands between a male and female is an old, little used form of marriage, though nowadays included as part of the marriage ritual by some groups.

Pilgrimages

Tirtha yatra – pilgrimages – are an essential aspect of Hinduism and are undertaken periodically. Reasons vary, from taking the ashes of ancestors to be submerged in the Ganges, in order to ask for a boon or in fulfilment of some desire. Pilgrimages may be made to any sacred place or to religious gatherings such as the Kumbha *Mela* (fair).

The Kumbha derives its name from the golden pitcher which contained the drink of immortality, four drops of which fell on four cities (see Chapter 11, Myths). This religious gathering is held in twelve-year cycles, that is, once every three years in the four cities of Nasik, Hardwar, Ujjain and Prayaga. The most important of these, Prayaga, carries the title of *tirthraja* (king of pilgrimages). The city is generally crowded with pilgrims but is overwhelmed by the millions who come for the special Kumbha Mela; the Prayaga is thought to be the largest religious festival in the world. Around

27 million people are estimated to have visited it in 1989, as it was considered the most auspicious occurrence in the last hundred and forty-four years.

The elderly participate in these pilgrimages. Indeed, many retire to sacred cities such as Varanasi and Haridwar, as there is a deep-seated belief that dying there will give them instant moksha.

Chapter 10

Sacred Texts & Liturgy

Traditionally, these texts are of of two kinds: *shruti* (heard), believed to be the direct word of God; and *smriti* (remembered), that is, that which has been formulated by humans. The teachings are ritually handed from teacher to disciple in the oral tradition even today (see page 41).

The *Shruti* Texts

The Veda seek to reveal the mystery of the universe with an incomparable richness and diversity. They appear as fresh and relevant today as they must have when they were first composed. They are broadly organized into four volumes – the *Rig-Veda* is the oldest and longest, with 1,028 verses. Some sources date it as early as 5000 BCE, although the text was probably compiled between 1300 and 1000 BCE. The *Rig-Veda* contains prayers for the common desire for longevity and prosperity. Most dramatically, it describes the origins of the universe. The *Yajur-Veda* gives accounts of

⊙ *Reading the sacred texts*

sacrificial procedures and the *Sama-Veda* contains chants. The fourth book, the *Atharva-Veda*, added much later, contains practical techniques, including the beginnings of Indian medical science.

Each of these Vedas has a foundational text, a *samhita* (collection) of verses and a prose text called the *brahmanas*. There are two further sections – the *aranyakas* and the *upanishads*. The aranyakas deal with the cosmic significance of Vedic rituals. They were probably meant for the hermit or forest-dweller who might not have had the wherewithal to perform the rituals in the same way as the householder.

Of the many upanishads, at least thirteen of the oldest are deemed to be Vedic – *Brhadaranayaka*, *Chandogya*, *Aitraya*, *Taittiriya*, *Isa*, *Kena*, *Katha*, *Prasna*, *Mundaka*, *Mandukya*, *Svetasvatara*, *Kaushitaki*, and *Maitri*. The upanishads are considered to be the last word on the Vedas, hence they are also known as *Vedanta*. The oldest upanishads are pre-Buddhist, although later texts may date from the beginning of the Common Era.

» *Isa Upanishad*, Verses 6–8

That which moves and yet does not move, That which is far away, That which is very near, That which is inside this world, That which is outside this all.

The one who sees all beings within oneself, and the same Self in all beings, feels no hatred, That Self will not seek to hide.

When in the being of the one of realization all beings become the very Self, what delusion, what sorrow can there be for the one who sees this Oneness?

The upanishads have a high cognitive content and reflect on the meaning of existence, the mystery of death and the nature of the universe. Their main message is that the deepest essence of all reality is the One Self, all-pervasive, and the divine source of the universe. It is identical with the innermost self of all beings and this is beautifully illustrated, for example, in the Isa upanishad. This upanishad forms part of the *Yajur-Veda* and takes its name from the opening word, *Isa* – God.

Mention here must also be made of the encyclopaedic works of *Charaka* (on medicine) and *Sushruta* (on surgery), compiled about 1000–800 BCE. They are regarded as the most authentic and renowned representative writings of the original *Ayurveda* (science of life). The *Ayurveda* is sometimes referred to as the fifth Veda.

The *Smriti* Texts

The *Smriti* are a vast collection of literature spanning many centuries. They contain the practical summaries of Hinduism and feature specialized traditions of learning – *shastras* (compositions) and *sutras* (essential ideas). They provide instructions for the proper pursuit of artha and dharma, including religious law, government, economics and the proper conduct of domestic ceremonies (marriage and funeral rituals), etc. One of the world's earliest manuals of polity, *Arthashastra* is attributed to Chandragupta Maurya's chief minister Kautilya. Even Sanskrit grammar is not overlooked.

Kama Sutra

The *Kama Sutra* must be one of the best-known book titles in the West. It deals with the quality of life. Sexual pleasure is only a part of *kama*, which is embraced as a proper human aim. The art of love as a whole is described. It includes a revealing discussion about a courtesan who was neither romanticized nor treated with contempt. Lovers of either sex are encouraged to show sensitivity and understanding towards their partners.

The Epics – *Ramayana* and *Mahabharata*

Perhaps the most celebrated, and certainly the most televised, works of Indian literature are the two great Sanskrit epics, the *Ramayana* and *Mahabharata* (great Bharat*). They are constructed around central stories and interwoven with a wealth of sub-plots, rhetoric and philosophy.

Ramayana

Composed by the poet Valmiki, the *Ramayana* is the story of Rama, the seventh incarnation of the god Vishnu, and a prince of the kingdom of Ayodhya. It recounts his education and his winning of the hand of Sita in marriage. Displaced as rightful heir to his father's throne, Rama goes into

* Bharat – land of the Bharata, a legendary figure and the name adopted for the Republic of India in 1947.

exile for fourteen years, accompanied by Sita and by his brother Lakshmana. Sita is abducted by the king of Sri Lanka, Ravana (although he was considered a demon by some people, he was in fact a highly accomplished and educated person).

With the aid of Hanuman and an army of monkeys, Rama, after a long search and many adventures, slays Ravana and rescues Sita. Rama installs Ravana's brother Vibhishina on the throne and returns to Ayodhya to regain his own throne and rules wisely.

Sita is accused of rumoured adultery during her captivity. Rama puts his duty to the people of his kingdom first and, although he believes Sita to be innocent, sends her into exile. Whilst sheltered by the hermit and poet Valmiki, she bears Rama's twin sons. After many years Rama and Sita are reunited. Rama, Sita, Lakshmana and Hanuman are revered as the quintessence of princely heroism, wifely and brotherly devotion, and loyal service, respectively.

Mahabharata

The *Mahabharata* is a different kind of story. It relates the conflict between two noble families, the Pandavas, led by their cousin Krishna, and their cousins the Kauravas. Set later than the *Ramayana,* traditionally around 3100 BCE, the struggle is ostensibly for possession of a worldly kingdom.

Hindus read it as the spiritual triumph of morality and justice. It is a large book which grips the reader at every point. Amongst the many stories and adventures, it describes a great Vedic ritual conducted by the head of the Pandava family.

The complexity, eloquence and rhetoric of the *Mahabharata* are exceptional even by today's standards. The most celebrated part of the *Mahabharata* is the *Bhagavad Gita,* although scholars argue that it was a later addition. It draws heavily on the teachings of the upanishads and the philosophy of Sankhya. It is a remarkable piece of work, beautifully conceived, combining philosophical subtlety with a precise literary style. Such is its power that almost every significant Hindu philosopher has written a commentary on it, and new translations and interpretations continue to appear.

The *Bhagavad Gita* takes the form of a dialogue between Krishna, in the role of a charioteer, and the Pandava hero Arjuna. At a dramatic moment just before the battle, Arjuna expresses his unwillingness to engage in a war against friends and relatives. Krishna's reply is a compelling argument. Arjuna must do his duty, as a Kshatriya, even though it may require killing, to uphold justice and morality. What follows is a brilliant spiritual metavision. Through Krishna the different approaches to life and spiritual development are revealed as complementary paths. Sacrifice and worldly duties, devotion, meditation and renunciation are all shown to have their place. Most dramatically of all, Arjuna is privileged to glimpse Krishna's awe-inspiring cosmic form before reverting to the familiar compassionate human form of Krishna.

There is much scholarly argument about the dates when the epics were composed. The *Ramayana* and the *Mababharata* were probably the result of many centuries of shaping before they reached their present written form between 300 BCE and 500 CE. Both these stories are embedded in a rich body of romantic, legendary tales and discourses on philosophy, law, geography, political science and astronomy. They are encyclopaedic, with the *Mahabharata* running to about 100,000 verses and the surviving text of the Ramayana totalling 24,000 verses.

The traditional sites of the *Mahabharata* are located in north-west India, whereas the traditional sites of the *Ramayana* are further to the east and south. To historians and archaeologists this is a puzzle. It is even possible that the *Ramayana* may be set before the Indo-Europeans came to India. The epics have inspired many further works. Of these, Tulsidas's *Ramayana* in Hindi is the most

popular. Reciting the *Ramayana* is considered a
religious act in its own right. Portions of it are
enacted annually, over a period of ten days, in
several places, including a major performance
held in Delhi.

The *Puranas*

Tradition attributes the *Mahabharata* to Vyasa, a
legendary *rishi* (sage) also said to be the compiler
of the *puranas*. The puranas are named so because
they are viewed as 'old'. The majority of the
puranas were probably compiled by many different
people between the fourth and the sixteenth
centuries CE. There are eighteen *mahapuranas*
(*maha* – great), extracted from a larger body of
puranic literature for special attention. All are
written in verse, and vary in length.

Perhaps more than any other literature,
traditional Hinduism, for the most part, is drawn
from the puranas. They are theistic and
predominantly sectarian in nature. Several expand
on themes found in the epics. They also popularize
the idea of *Trimurti*, the three aspects of one God –
Brahma, Vishnu and Shiva. Five topics distinguish
the genuine purana. These are: the creation,
destruction and recreation of the universe; the
history of humankind; the genealogy of the gods

and sages; descriptions of the Manus; and the history of the lunar and solar dynasties.

In addition to these categories ot literature, there are many other works which have contributed to the development of Hindu culture. There are, for example, medieval texts such as the *Hathapradipika,* one of the most famous texts to emerge from the great Nath school of yoga. The original author, *Svatmarama Swami,* was from a notable line of medieval yogis who traced their teaching back to the Mahayogi Gorakshanath. It contains a deep understanding of human psychosomatic functions and describes powerful traditional methods used to awaken a human being's vast potential.

Chapter 11

Myths

The use of the word 'myth' as a false notion or a fabrication does not apply in Hinduism. Myths in this context are traditional stories of ostensibly historical events and cosmology which accentuate meanings rather than facts. They provide metaphors for deep spiritual truths which may be interpreted at different levels in the tradition of parables. Mythical language uses symbols, poetic images, similes and allegories not only to make the stories more attractive but to convey a philosophy rooted in mystical experience. They contain practical guidance for individuals, thus they serve to safeguard and reinforce moral order.

Each of the following myths has alternative versions. Like facets of a crystal, myths may be viewed from different perspectives. They are given different readings and retold, rediscovered and reinterpreted even today. Hindus recognize the contemporary relevance of the stories and generally accept the revisions stemming from social developments.

⊙ *Kartikeya – one of the sons of Shiva*

Creation Myth

The universe is said to have come into being when
Indra (king of gods and rain) cleaved out heaven and
earth from a singularity. Indra then erected a great
pillar to prop heaven and earth apart, providing a
space in between. This pillar is conceived as the axis
of the world. In some myths it is Shiva's linga.
Vishnu contributed to cosmic development, in his
incarnation as a dwarf, by iterating three worlds
(*bhur, bhuvah, sva*) while making three giant steps.

In the beginning, the universe appeared as chaos. Out of the chaos desire (which led to change) was born. Prajapati (champion of creatures) was the first being and a hermaphrodite. Four sons were born from the female side – fire, wind, sun and moon and a daughter called Usha (dawn). Prajapati desired his daughter and committed incest with her. She fled from him and hid in the form of a doe, so he became a stag. She became a mare and he a horse, she a cow and he a bull and in this way all the species were created. Thus the myths convey the powerful notion of recursion. The gods, shocked by this impropriety, created Rudra (god of storms and the Vedic antecedent of Shiva), to punish Prajapati.

Another myth relates how Brahma the creator produced the first king of India, Manu Svayambhu (self-born Man). He was a hermaphrodite and, from the female half, gave birth to two sons and three daughters. A number of Manus descended from the sons, the first of whom was called Prithu. He became king, then cleared the forests and cultivated the land, created systems and looked after all creatures. The earth is called Prithvi after him. During the time of the seventh Manu there was a great flood. Vishnu had warned Manu of the flood and told him to build a boat and save his family, the seven *rishis* and two each of every living being. Vishnu then incarnated as a giant fish and guided the boat to a mountain, where it was lodged until the flood subsided.

Incarnations of Vishnu

Vishnu is supposed to have twenty-two *avatars* (incarnations), of which ten (see overleaf) are the best known. Of these, nine incarnations have already occurred; the tenth and last is yet to come.

Many Hindus believe that modern saint-like figures across the cultural divide are avatars, for example Ramakrishna, Jesus and, more recently, Mahatma Gandhi. Indeed, Gandhi himself had endorsed the doctrine and referred to Jesus as an avatar.

Churning of the Ocean of Milk

A puranic story which has its roots in Vedic times tells how the *asura* (dark beings) were gaining ascendancy. The *sura* (beings of light) decided they needed an advantage: obtaining *amrita* (life-giving drink) and thus achieving immortality. Amrita was to be extracted from the ocean of milk (the undifferentiated cosmos from which everything emerged). As this proved to be very a difficult task, after many attempts the sura enlisted the help of the demons to churn the ocean, promising them a share of the amrita.

❱❱ *Avatars* (Incarnations) of Vishnu

Matsya a giant fish – Vishnu saved the seventh Manu and all the species of the world from the great flood

Kamatha (or Kurma) he took the form of a tortoise during the churning of the ocean

Varahain in the form of a boar he destroyed demons and rescued the Earth when it fell from its place

Narasimha the man-lion who disembowelled the demon *Hiranyakashap* , after which the festival of Holi is celebrated

Vamana the demon Bali had conquered the universe and Vishnu incarnated as Vamana the dwarf who begged for enough land to lie on, or as much as he could cover in three strides. Bali foolishly agreed and Vishnu strode across in a gigantic form to trick him out of the entire universe

Parshurama also known as Rama of the axe. He beheaded his unchaste mother and then destroyed the entire class of Kshatriyas to avenge his father, a Brahmin. He was later granted a boon to bring his mother back to life

Rama hero of the *Ramayana* epic

Krishna hero of the *Mahabharata* epic and voice of the *Bhagavad Gita*. He promised to incarnate whenever righteousness waned

Buddha he incarnated as Buddha to teach that the orthodox claim was a false doctrine to delude pious demons

Kalki Vishnu will finally appear as the rider on the white horse, come to destroy the universe at the end of the age of Kali. This is sometimes represented as a white horse that awaits its rider

The Mandara mountain was used as the churning pole and Vasuki, the great serpent, as the rope to turn it. The agitation caused by the churning threatened to shatter the world so they invoked Vishnu's help. Vishnu transformed himself into a tortoise and supported the pole on his back, providing a firm base. As the ocean became agitated a number of treasures came forth, including Lakshmi, the goddess of wealth, who married Vishnu, and Kamadhenu (the sacred cow which provides wealth). A virulent poison that threatened to destroy mankind also appeared. Shiva alone, immortal among the gods, drank the poison. Rather than completely swallowing it, he stored it in his throat, which turned blue. Thus he is also called Neelkantha (blue throat).

Eventually, the amrita appeared, provoking a struggle between the gods and the demons. During the commotion four drops of the amrita fell on four cities – Prayaga, Hardwar, Nasik and Ujjain. The demons managed to secure the amrita, leaving the gods to beg Vishnu for help again. This time Vishnu transformed himself into Mohini, a beautiful temptress, and tricked the demons into giving her the amrita to dispose of as she pleased. Thus the gods obtained immortality.

In one interpretation of this myth, the ocean represents the primordial nature of the universe. The levels of the mind are represented by the mountain which is immersed in the ocean. The serpent represents the dynamics of time and process. The churning symbolizes the constructive processes of the mind. The preliminary gifts represent the forms of experience brought forth. This may include higher blissful states of consciousness and attaining *siddhis* (competences). The resulting product, amrita, represents moksha. However, attachment to such things is dangerous. They must be held in abeyance if transcendent reality is to be realized.

Creation of Goddesses

There was a demon called Manishasura (*man* – mind, + *ish* – to move away, thus someone who has lost touch with humanity). He performed a long penance and successfully prayed to Shiva to obtain the boon of invincibility. Naturally, Manishasura became all-powerful and defeated the gods. This made them very angry and from the combined energies of their fury emerged a goddess. She was given the name of Durga (impassable) and, empowered with weapons donated by each of the gods, she confronted Manishasura and destroyed him. She is particularly popular in Bengal, where she is depicted as Shiva's wife.

Durga was called Sati (pure) in her incarnation as the daughter of Daksha (the righteous one). After fasting regularly, she eventually attained Shiva as her

⊙ Kali, the hideous, terrifying aspect of the goddess Durga, Shiva's wife

husband. Subsequently, Daksha held a major ritual to which all the gods except Shiva were invited. The gods were afraid that Daksha would become all-powerful if this yajna was completed and thus prevailed upon Shiva to prevent it. Shiva devised a clever plan and persuaded Sati to attend the function. Thus provoked, Daksha could not resist insulting her husband and her remarks so incensed Sati that she resolved not to remain in a body derived from her father. She threw herself on the sacred fire during the ceremony, now void. When Shiva found out he snatched her half-burnt body from the flames and in his grief would not let her go. Temples dedicated to her arose wherever parts of her body fell in the macabre dance throughout India that followed.

This dance of death is depicted in an inverted form at the Kalighata temple in Calcutta. The goddess Kali in her hideous black aspect dances upon the corpse of her husband, Shiva. In doing so she animates him by changing the *shava* (corpse) into Shiva, the living god. This terrifying aspect of Kali is balanced by her maternal aspect as Gauri, the fair one. Shiva once taunted Kali for being dark. Ashamed, she performed many austerities and as the result of a boon was able to slough off her dark skin, which took the form of Kali. The symbolism here is an obvious one as it reminds us of the positive and negative aspects of our own personality.

A question often asked in connection with Kali is about the Thugs and whether they still exist. They were a secret organization of robbers active just before the Muslim conquest. They saw themselves as 'Robin Hood'-like characters, although this is a moot point. Legends grew up about their exploits, the basis for many adventure novels and films.

The Thugs were devotees of Kali in some of her more alarming forms. They regarded their activities as religious rituals. Included in their ranks were many respectable elements, though there is little doubt that criminal elements (both Hindu and Muslim) also participated, particularly in the early period of the British Raj. They usually met in October, in bands of 10 to 200. They lay in wait near the highways, where they would set upon wealthy travellers and strangle them with a cloth (though they would never harm women). A portion of their takings was always offered to Kali in one of her temples. Around 1829, a campaign against them was started and was remarkably successful. Within seven years over three thousand of them had been imprisoned or hanged and the Thugs were effectively wiped out.

Krishna

Krishna is one of the most popular of gods. He was originally a dark deity from South India, who is now identified with the Krishna of the *Mahabharata*.

⊙ *Krishna, hero of the* Mahabharata *epic and his beloved Radha*

He incarnated to kill his wicked uncle, King Kansa.
Kansa knew that he would be killed by his nephew,
so he imprisoned his sister and brother-in-law in
order to kill any male offspring. Yet, when Krishna
was born the prison locks miraculously opened and
Krishna's father was able to smuggle him out of the
palace. Exchanged with the daughter of a simple
cow-herd in a nearby kingdom, he was brought up
tending cows. When Kansa discovered this he
killed the little girl and ordered the slaughter of all
new-born boys in his kingdom.

The mischievous Krishna was full of fun and was
dearly loved by the *gopis* (cow-herd women). He did

many extraordinary deeds both secretly and publicly. Once he dived into a river, ostensibly to rescue a ball, but his real intention was to get rid of Kalya (black), the wicked serpent, who was tormenting the villagers. During the battle that ensued Krishna became dark through encountering Kalya's fetid breath.

Krishna was charming, gallant and a skilled politician. His adventures are recounted in some of the Puranas but particularly in the *Mahabharata*. Eventually, he did kill Kansa and slew many other demons. (After many battles the whole of his clan, who had become degenerate, killed each other in the fulfilment of a sage's curse). Krishna himself was accidently killed by a hunter, who, mistaking him for a deer, shot him in the foot, his only vulnerable spot. Kaliyuga, the fourth and current age, commenced with Krishna's death.

Diwali

A poor fisherman found a priceless necklace in the stomach of a fish. It was the queen's favourite jewel, which she had lost whilst bathing in the river. The clever fishwife coached her husband and told him to take the necklace to the palace. 'Refuse any reward offered' she said, 'but when the king insists, ask that on a certain day in October, no house but ours is allowed to be illuminated.'

When opportunity, in the form of Lakshmi, came to the locality, she was attracted to the fisherman's house. It was the only one the goddess of wealth could find when she needed a home. Every year, since that day, people clean and decorate their homes and put lighted candles, oil lamps and lanterns everywhere to attract Lakshmi. It pays to be ready.

Holi

The demon king Hiraranyakashap had been granted a wish by Shiva – 'that neither man nor beast would destroy him, neither could he be killed in the house nor outdoors, neither on earth nor in the skies, neither at night nor in the daytime.' Assured of his own immortality (and the validity of excluded middle logic) Hiraranyakashap proclaimed he was God. His son Prahalad would not accept the divinity of his father and incurred his murderous wrath.

After many unsuccessful murder attempts, Hiraranyakashap enlisted the aid of his sister Holika, who had been granted immunity from fire as the result of a minor boon. A great fire was lit, and in front of a huge crowd, Holika jumped into it, clasping Prahalad in her arms. Prahalad prayed to Vishnu, who immediately incarnated as Narasimha – a human-lion being, who was neither man nor beast. At dusk, Narasimha sat in the doorway of the palace with the king on his knees, and killed him by disembowelling him with his claws, thus, meeting the terms of the boon and promoting the power of creative thought.

Unfortunately, Holika had neglected the fact that her immunity was valid only if she entered a fire alone. She was burnt alive but happily Prahalad emerged unharmed through the protection of Vishnu. The crowd celebrated by throwing coloured powder. Whilst things may seem clear in black and white, there really are colourful alternatives. The festival of Holi is named after Holika and involves a celebratory bonfire.

Chapter 12

Reform & Modern Movements

Examples of New Movements

The following list is not comprehensive, but includes some of the better known movements. Many of them have branches and followers in the West.

Brahmo Samaj

Brahmo Samaj (society of Brahma) was founded in 1828 by Ram Mohan Roy (1772–1833), a Bengali Brahmin in Calcutta. It is monotheistic and rejects the use of images. Ram Mohan Roy believed in social reform, the rights of women and was instrumental in the abolition of the practice of *sati* (see below).

Swami Narayan

The Swami Narayan movement traces its teachings to the philosopher Ramanuja, but was given a fresh impetus in the early nineteenth century by Sahajanada. Sahajananda was born in

⊙ *Followers of Hari Krishna*

Uttar Pradesh but settled in Gujarat. The movement encourages charitable works such as the building of hospitals. It joined in the opposition to sati, and supported the right of young widows to remarry. The majority of its followers are from the Gujarati community.

Arya Samaj

Arya Samaj (society of Aryans) was founded in 1875 by a Brahmin, Dayananda Sarasvati. He was brought up in a Shaivite home. As a young boy he once stayed up all night in order to celebrate the twenty-four-hour fast of *Shivaratri* (Shiva's night). Late that night when all was quiet, he watched a mouse nibbling at the offerings to Shiva. This led him to question the whole notion of idol worship and ritual. He advocated a return to the pure tradition of the Veda and preached a synthesis of Vedic ideals with modern ideas. Arya Samaj believes in equal opportunity and has founded many colleges and schools.

Ramakrishna

Ramakrishna Mission was established by a Vendantist, Swami Vivekananda, in the late nineteenth century. The inspiration came from Ramakrishna, who was a Bengali Brahmin in the bhakti tradition. He preached that all religions led to God, but he himself remained a lifelong devotee of Kali, as the Cosmic Mother. The mission has branches in many countries. It teaches non-dualism and carries out many educational, cultural and social activities.

Dr Ambedkar

Mention must be made here of Dr Ambedkar. (1891–1956). He was born in 1891 in a Dalit household and was a victim of social discrimination. In due course, his brilliance brought him to the notice of the Maharaja of

Baroda, who sent him abroad to study law. He was part of the Round Table Conferences with the British, which produced a Constitution for India in 1947. He secured a large reservation of seats for the scheduled classes in the Parliament. As the first Law Minister he was largely responsible for enacting India's Constitution. However, he was never convinced that discrimination against the scheduled classes would be overcome. Just before he died in 1956, he converted to Buddhism, which he saw as an Indian religion. Around 600,000 of his followers converted with him.

Divine Light Society and Others

Amongst the many movements initiated in the twentieth century, the Divine Light Society was founded in 1932 by Sivananda, a medical doctor. It did much to popularize Hatha Yoga in the West, as has the impetus provided by B. K. S. Iyengar. More devotionally inclined, the International Society for Krishna Consciousness better known as the Hari Krishna movement, was started in the USA in 1966 by Swami Prabhupada.

Gurus

Following in the god-men (and -women) tradition there has always been a generous supply of gurus. Sai Baba of the broad smile and Afro-style haircut, is believed to be a living god by his six (some estimate it as ten) million followers worldwide. Maharishi Mahesh Yogi (of Beatles fame), Ma Nirmala Devi and Bhagwan Rajneesh are some of the other media-minded (self-styled) gurus.

» Hindu Assembly

The nearest equivalent to a central authority is the Hindu Mahasabha (Great Assembly). It meets several times a year, particularly during festivals such as the Kumbha Mela. It is comprised of many ascetic orders and sectarian groups, who tend to be orthodox and conventional. In reality, however, it is a political organization and has no real way of monitoring or regulating the diverse groups.

New Gods/Goddesses

In Hinduism there is no formal process of beatification and canonization as may be found in certain Christian denominations. However, new gods and goddesses continue to emerge, in recent years notably Santoshi Mata, launched on Hinduism by Bollywood in a film called *Jai* (hail) *Santoshi Mata*. It is claimed that she is the daughter of Ganesha and his wife Riddhi-Siddhi, being thereby the grand-daughter of Shiva and Parvati. Despite objections raised by a few Vedic priests about her precedence, the fact that she has obtained a genealogy places her firmly in the Hindu pantheon. She has her own set of success stories, special prayers and incantations, and now a following of millions, who find her perfectly credible.

Sati

Ordinary people may also be elevated. The eighteen-year-old Roop Kanwar became another kind of goddess in a small village in Rajasthan. She attracted international media attention in 1987 when she burnt herself on the funeral pyre of her husband. She became *sati* and her action was defended, mostly but not exclusively, by vested interests and men, who proclaimed she was a goddess. Her village is now thriving materially as the site of her death has become a shrine attracting thousands of visitors every year.

Outlawed in the nineteenth century, today the practice of sati seems to be moribund but not quite defunct, as forty such deaths have been officially recorded since India became independent. The practice is not mentioned in the Vedas. The practice may have been introduced by the Scytho-Tartars but such origins are questionable. The Rajput princesses certainly burnt themselves rather than fall into the hands of the conquering Muslims. The practice appears to have been given a spurious religious sanction by the mythological story of Sati.

Hinduism Today

The impact of films and television in a country where half the population is illiterate cannot be underestimated. For the general public in India, if it is on television then it must definitely be true. The televised version of the two epics, *Ramayana* and *Mahabharata,* eighty or ninety episodes each, was seen by over a 100 million viewers, quite irrespective of religion. The actors and actresses depicting the main characters are accepted by many as the real manifestations of the gods and goddesses they portrayed. Their touch is alleged to heal and their followers believe the actors have the power to fulfil wishes. When some of these actors (in common with certain Hollywood personalities) entered politics they experienced landslide victories in the elections.

Contentious situations such as the temple/mosque incident in Ayodhya (a city in the north-east and the alleged birthplace of Rama) are more serious. The origins of the problem can be traced to Babar (the first Mughal ruler of India, c. 1526), who had a mosque built on the original site of a temple dedicated to Rama. Some years ago, the mosque was torn down by fundamentalists who wanted Rama's temple rebuilt. This story not only made international news, but was seen across most of India, including many previously isolated areas. Thus local issues can now excite wider populations and provoke more problems. The site is heavily guarded and the dispute has still not been resolved. Periodically, politicians may use this to their advantage. Old television recordings and other media showing brawling scenes can stimulate coordinated communal rioting when required.

At its core Hinduism is perhaps one of the greatest and most profound religions of the world. Yet there is a huge gap which separates its highest spiritual understanding from localized superstitious practices. As a living religion it continues to evolve and adapt to meet the needs of its followers. The current social and cultural changes, political upheavals and widespread corruption in India make it difficult to evaluate the changes that are taking place in Hinduism. There has been a movement away from the main tenet of Hinduism – the importance of fulfilling one's duty (*dharma*) – towards the demanding of rights. Most Hindus brought up with traditional values find this and the widespread *adharma* (corrupt practices) extremely stressful but have a fatalistic approach to the problem. They, like Arjuna, take comfort from the words of Krishna:

'Being unborn, my Spirit is imperishable.
As God of all beings and established in creation,
I incarnate by my spiritual power. For whenever
dharma declines, Arjuna, and adharma grows
strong, then do I generate an embodied Self.
For the protection of the righteous, and
the destruction of unrighteousness, and for
the establishment of virtue I take birth age
after age.'

Chapter 4, verses 6–8 of the Gita

Endnote

A written text is a linear exposition and a necessary choice of words must reveal some meanings whilst leaving other interpretations unstated. This is unavoidable in a book of this length. It is hoped that the reader will continue where this account must stop. The reader is left to the grand adventure, which is no less than the discovery of oneself in everything and the universe in oneself. This is encapsulated in the essence of the Veda – *aham Brahmasmi* (I am Brahman) and *aham tat sat* (I am That).

Glossary

*A guide to the pronunciation of the Sanskrit words
is given in parentheses.
ä = as in pass; š̃ = as in shall*

ahimsa – non-violence

amrita – life-giving fluid

aparigraha – non-grasping

arti (ärati) – ceremony consisting of waving a
lighted lamp in front of the *murti* (image of a deity)
as an offering of light

ashram – stage, resting-place

artha – acceptance of wealth, possession and
power – the objects of worldly activity

arya (ärya) – noble or honourable

Atharva-Veda – the Fourth Veda

atma – self, inner self, consciousness, sometimes
erroneously translated as 'soul'. It comes from the
Rig-Vedic term for 'breath'

Ayurveda – science of life

Bhagavad Gita – song of God

bhakti – devotion

bhur – material realm

bhuvah – bioenergetic realm

bindu or bindi – dot, globule, drop, the mark on the forehead symbolizing the third eye of wisdom; in metaphysical terms nothingness, zero

brahamchari – student

Brahma – as the creator, the first member of Trimurti

Brahman – the Supreme, One without a second, the Singularity

brahmacharya – sexual restraint, continence

Brahmin – a member of one of the four hereditary groups and traditionally includes historians, educators, priests

dakshina – a kind of levy or fee given to the priest

dalit – the oppressed

darshana – perspectives, insight, also view

dharma – righteousness

dharmic – righteous

dvija – twice born

grihastha – householder

gunas – quality/string

triguna – three substantial qualities that emerge from an unmanifest, transcendental state

Ishvara – God; in sectarian movements the title of the creator of the universe

jnana – knowledge (pronounced 'gyan' – *g* as in girl, *y* as in yam and *an* as in ann)

jati – intermarrying family group (from *ja* – born or begotten, also *jar* – root)

Kali (Käli) – the most wrathful form of the goddess Durga, also called Kali Ma. She represents the destructive aspects of 'mother' nature

kaliyuga – the fourth and present age, started when Krishna died

kama – achieving quality of life in a balanced way, not hedonism

karma – action

kshatriya – a member of the hereditary group that traditionally includes kings, warriors and technologists

Lakshmi – Vishnu's female partner

linga – the (male) creative organ

maha – great

mahasabha – the great assembly

Manu – there are many Manus; the first human being, an ancient law-giver and the founding fathers of humankind

moksha – the ultimate goal; liberation from the cycle of births and deaths *mrita* – death

murti – material form, image of a deity

nirguna – without attributes

prakriti – concept of nature, the source of the material world

puja – worship

puranas – old, 'stories of,' traditional texts

purusha – broadly, the concept of consciousness

rajas – activity

rangoli – diagram or pattern created, generally by women, on the ground in front of their homes on special occasions; particularly popular in South India

Rig-Veda – the oldest and longest of the Vedas, with 1,028 verses

saguna – with attributes

samadhi – complete absorption/identification

Sama-Veda – the second of the Vedas

sannyasi – one who has renounced worldly things

sanskaras – memory constructions, also rites of passage

Sarasvati – the goddess of learning, Brahma's female partner

sati – pure

sattva – actuality

satya – truth

Shaivism – the worship of Shiva

shakti – power

shasfras – compositions

Shiva (Sivä) – one of the trinity of gods, the completer or destroyer

Shudras – member of hereditary group that traditionally includes workers

smriti – remembered

shraddha (šraddha) – respect

shruti (šruti) – heard, revelation

sutras – string, sometimes used as a summary name for aphorisms

sva – cognitive realm

tamas – potentiality

tantra – roughly translates as 'web' and represents the idea of a phenomenal world woven by the complex interplay of order and chaos

Tantric yoga – a spiritual path whose practitioners believe that the purpose of life is to embrace the whole of life itself

trimurti – three images. Symbolizes three aspects of a singular God

Vaishnavites – followers of Vishnu

vaishya – a member of the hereditary group that

traditionally includes agriculturists and artisans, traders and money-lenders

vanaprastha – one who has retired from active life

varna – segment, category, colour

veda – knowledge, from the root *vid* – to know. Veda is the summary name for a collection of scriptures sacred to the Hindus

Vishnu – the second of the trinity of gods, as the sustainer of the universe

Yajur-Veda – the second Veda

yajna – sacrifice, worship by making an offering to the gods, sacrament

Further Reading

A History of India, Vol. 1, Romila Thapar, Penguin, 1990.

A History of India, Vol. 2, Percival Spear, Penguin, 1990.

A Popular Dictionary of Hinduism, Karel Werner, Curzon Press, 1994.

Gods, Demons and Others, R.K. Narayan, Vision Books, 1987.

Hindu Myths, Wendy Doniger O'Flaherty, Penguin, 1994.

Hinduism, Nirad Chaudhri, Chatto & Windus, 1979.

Hindus, Julius Lipner, Routledge, 1995.

Mahabharata, Kamala Subramaniam, Bharata Vidya Bhavan, 1988.

Shrimad Valmiki Ramayana, N.Raghunathan, Vighneshwar, 1981.

The Principal Upanishads, S. Radhakrishnan, George Allen & Unwin, 1953.

The Vedic Experience, Raimundo Pannikar, University of California Press, 1977.

The Wonder That Was India, A.L. Basham, New York, 1959.

The Concise Srimad Bhagavatam, Swami Venkatesananda, State University of New York Press, 1989.

Index